Understanding & Counseling THE MISBEHAVING STUDENT

By John F. Taylor, Ph.D

Understanding & Counseling The Misbehaving Student

10-DIGIT ISBN: 1-57543-175-0
13-DIGIT ISBN: 978-1-57543-175-8

Published by mar*co products, inc.
1443 Old York Road
Warminster, PA 18974
1-800-448-2197
www.marcoproducts.com

Graphics from: www.shutterstock.com

PRINTED IN THE U.S.A.

CONTENTS

Understanding & Counseling THE MISBEHAVING STUDENT

Introduction

Problematic conduct in students can reflect misbehavior, malfunctioning, or both.

Misbehavior and malfunctioning usually reflect psychological mechanisms that can be detected by a supervising adult—a teacher, caregiver, counselor, or parent. This book provides these adults with guidelines for helping any student participate more fully and successfully at school, in any grade. It includes:

- key principles for understanding why students misbehave
- effective activities that teachers, counselors, administrators, and students can use to help decrease incidents of conflict at school
- suggestions for recognizing and understanding root causes of misbehavior in order to meet the student's emotional needs and prevent further adjustment difficulties

This guidebook is directed primarily toward school counselors, mental health professionals, parent educators, teachers, parents, and others who assist children and adolescents with behavioral difficulties. As you use this guidebook, simply translate *the adult* into *me* and *student* into the *child* or *adolescent* about who I am concerned.

CHAPTER 1

Understanding & Counseling
The Misbehaving Student

School-Centered Misbehavior

This guidebook focuses on students whose needs are not being fully met at school or at home. Poor performance and malfunctioning reflect unmet needs. Underproductive and uncooperative students give evidence of needfulness in many ways.

Search for malfunctioning in four major areas:

Receptivity
Participation
Behavior Control
Productivity

While not a comprehensive listing of all possible warning signals for student misbehavior, the chart on page 11 lists common indications that distinguish needful students from fully participating classmates.

Receptivity Of Instruction:

- require repetition of the teacher's remarks
- require one-to-one instruction
- don't take good lecture notes
- don't pay attention

Participation:

- avoid joining class discussions
- avoid raising their hands
- contribute few ideas
- interject wisecracks and irrelevant ideas

Behavior Control:

- display disruptive behavior to:
  - draw negative teacher attention
  - show off to classmates
- get into fights before or after school or at recess
- annoy classmates
- describe school in derogatory terms
- deface the building and damage school property

Productivity:

- take tests in a careless, indifferent manner
- turn in incomplete or carelessly done homework
- give up quickly on challenging tasks
- produce poor-quality seatwork
- produce poor-quality homework
- don't prepare well for tests
- turn in assignments late
- do not do assigned seatwork or homework

Energy Level Is A Key Factor

All of the student's efforts at absorbing stresses, performing, producing schoolwork, conforming to adult expectations, and coping with the rigors of life take energy. When there is too much to cope with and too little energy available, path-of-least-resistance behavior emerges. The lower the student's overall energy level, the less resilient the student is to stress, and the more likely it is that he/she will have trouble resisting temptations and putting a rein on anger. Even though stresses may seem legitimate—as in such commonplace activities as doing homework or chores, practicing a musical instrument, or simply being courteous to others—the student is more likely to misbehave if the total energy demand exceeds the energy available for coping.

Understood from this perspective, misbehavior can be recognized as a deteriorated level of functioning based, in part, on lowered coping energy for self-actualization and self-control. Useful energy has been sidetracked into basic coping. Any factors that decrease the student's available energy are suspect.

Among the most common are playing videogames and watching television. Others include deficiencies in overall health, body weight, stamina, bedroom disarray, sleep quality, dietary habits, and related factors. The use of chemicals that reduce the body's efficiency also leads to increased likelihood of misbehavior. Alcohol, marijuana, tobacco products, and drugs fall into this category.

Children who are emotionally overburdened for any reason consistently have low energy for coping. To fully develop emotional health and coping skills, children need to feel protected and sheltered from stresses in general and from potentially overwhelming stresses in particular. A key component of effective parenting is providing an umbrella-like filter against otherwise traumatic or overwhelming emotional demands.

Children should be able to develop confidence that their reasonable needs will be met and that it is safe to relax, play, and be at ease about life. Children who are emotionally overburdened must face adult-level challenges relatively unfiltered by what essentially are leaky parental stress umbrellas.

Any factors that decrease the student's available energy are suspect.

The result is that these children develop self-protective insulation. Unfortunately, their substitutes are never as effective as a good parent-supplied stress umbrella would have been.

The following telltale signs of emotional overburdening may occur singly or in combination. The more intensely they are acted-out, the greater the reflection of the student's emotional overburdening.

Emotional Hardness

The student goes into a survival mode, becoming emotionally numb and unempathic. Insensitive to the needs and concerns of others, the student essentially lives by the secret self-talk motto:

> *"I don't care about others. All my energy has to go for personal survival."*

Abnormal Need To Control

The student tries to maintain a dominant position in virtually all interpersonal relationships, including those with authority figures. The student won't tolerate being in any situation that would lead to being caught in a one-down position or result in any kind of personal vulnerability. Evidence of this abnormal need to control reflects an attempt to be safe by ensuring that nobody can hurt him/her.

> *"If I can control them, they can't hurt me."*

The need for excessive control is a spinoff of the need to feel safe from harm.

Evidences of such a need include:

- giving evasive answers
- telling people what they want to hear rather than the truth
- not admitting personal weakness or error
- telling elaborate lies and mingling truth with falsehood
- refusing to divulge personal information
- bullying
- violating others' boundaries, such as privacy and property rights
- acting-out in sneaky ways

Avoidance Of Responsibilities

The student believes that assertion would not result in his/her needs being met. In order to be relieved of feeling the sting of having unmet needs, the student represses awareness of feelings and loses the determination to strive, cope, or care about anything. This form of self-protective insulation shields the student by providing a disconnect from reality and from feeling responsible to interact with the environment.

Low resilience to any burden or stress brings with it a tendency to evade a high percentage of ordinary demands from adults. The student stops participating at school and withdraws into a seemingly endless parade of sensually pleasant, frivolous preoccupations.

Malfunction Doesn't Necessarily Mean *Misbehavior*

Just because a student's needs aren't being met doesn't mean the student will necessarily misbehave.

Three basic options are available. The student may do nothing at all to address the situation and simply try to keep functioning despite remaining needful. These lose–lose non-assertions usually lead to *malfunctioning,* but not to *misbehavior.*

The second option is to make assertions that don't do a satisfactory job of meeting the underlying needs they are intended to address. These lose–lose assertions are *misbehavior.*

The third option is to make positive, socially appropriate assertions that result in win–win events and fulfill the underlying needs. Consider the student who is throwing paper wads, cracking jokes, and interrupting classmates with wisecracks. This student has an obvious need to feel a greater degree of social enmeshment.

Lose–Lose Non-Assertion

The first option, a lose–lose non-assertion, would amount to going to school, sitting at the desk, and feeling the sting of social rejection and unpopularity. The student would take no action to improve social enmeshment. The result would probably be a depression-like stupor of inability to address the tasks at hand. There would be no *misbehavior*—just *malfunctioning.* But the malfunctioning would be every bit as crippling, if not more so, than the misbehavior resulting from the second option. The student loses and so do his/her classmates. Lose–lose non-assertion leads to *malfunctioning.*

Lose–Lose Assertion

If the student chooses the second option of misbehaving, the socially inappropriate assertions don't enhance social enmeshment and the quality of friendships with classmates. They gain the student only fleeting moments of being noticed by peers and teachers, who gradually become increasingly aggravated by his/her silly antics. The student loses and his/her classmates lose. Lose–lose assertion amounts to *misbehavior.*

Win–Win Assertion

The third option—socially appropriate assertions to enhance social enmeshment in healthy ways—might include reading a book on how to make and keep friends, helping a teacher as an aide for younger students, joining a club or social group where new friends could be made, and similar activities. The student wins and others win. Socially appropriate assertion leads to win–win results.

Maladaptive vs. Assertion

Imagine this scene: The teacher presents seatwork of moderate difficulty with a clear intention of seeing that every student performs it diligently. Student Jane feels overwhelmed by the difficulty level of the seatwork. Now we have a problem. The teacher's expectations don't match the student's readiness to perform. The teacher has expectations, and Jane has a need to feel strong and competent in spite of the obvious, direct threat to her sense of competence. The stage is set for Jane to be uncooperative.

Any child or teen whose needs are not met has only three options. In our example, Jane needs to feel self-confident. Her first option doesn't involve misbehaving. The student tries to perform and participate, but remains needful. The result is a *malfunction.* In our example, Jane would attempt the seatwork, but quickly become frustrated. Rather than misbehave, she might stare out the window and feel incompetent. Maybe a tear trickles down her cheek as she thinks of how unable she is to rise to the level the teacher expects. She might think of how her older brother gets higher grades and how disappointed her parents have been in her. *Depression* is just a small step from how Jane is feeling. She is *malfunctioning.* Though not purposely *misbehaving,* she is certainly *underproductive.*

Her second option is to misbehave in an attempt to sidestep the sting of the needfulness. But how will she show her uncooperativeness? One way to feel less needful is to pretend not to be interested in doing the seatwork. Another way is to distract the teacher and provide temporary excitement by throwing paper wads or bothering a neighboring student. While these behaviors have a cost in terms of incurring whatever irritation the teacher displays or consequences the teacher enforces, misbehavior is an attractive option. It provides a temporary sense of personal strength in situations in which the student actually feels vulnerable, weak, or incompetent. Misbehavior always has a power core. The misbehaving student always feels more powerful.

These first two options are *maladaptive.* They represent faulty choices. Students choose to malfunction or they choose to misbehave. Nobody is making them choose either option. They are in control of their own actions. Both reflect a great deal of personally experienced pain, mostly psychological and emotional. Both of them create lose–lose results; the student loses and the teacher loses. Classmates and parents also lose.

This book focuses on students who are choosing either of these maladaptive options in lieu of the third, and by far the best, option. Your goal is always to assist students at any grade level in rejecting the first two options. Then the way is open to help them make the wisest choice of all, and the only one of the three that creates win–win results.

Jane can resolve this situation with a third option. She can choose *assertion* of her needs. She could assert to classmates by asking a friend to help her with the assignment. She can directly ask the teacher for help and clarification. She can ask for more time to complete the assignment. She can ask her parents to help her at home, or to go with her to talk with her guidance counselor about changing to a less-demanding class. She could utilize a commercially available study guide from a bookstore or library to enhance her competence.

Socially appropriate assertion, like the other two options, has drawbacks and risks. What if the teacher doesn't respond in a caring and alert fashion to Jane's appeals for help? Worse yet, what if the teacher gives an inconsiderate, hostile, angry, or punitive answer to Jane? Or what if the teacher responds courteously, but can't understand why Jane is having problems doing the work? What if the teacher's advice and explanations still don't solve the problem of Jane's incompetence at performing the task? What if the other students don't like Jane and aren't interested in helping her? What if her parents don't assist and criticize her for being lazy or stupid? What if her guidance counselor doesn't agree to discuss switching classes, or decides against any changes in curriculum? What if the study guide from the bookstore is just as confusing as the textbook? If assertion doesn't eliminate the needfulness, Jane has only two options left. Both are *maladaptive.*

Misbehavior Is Always An Attempt At Need-Meeting

Any student's misbehavior always has interpersonal or intrapersonal (within the self) causes and consequences. It is usually the end product of faulty perceptions, faulty reasoning, or not-so-faulty perception of an emotionally stressful circumstance. It reflects several factors, including family relationships, self-concept, relationships with peers, sibling and family issues, and such physiological factors as fatigue and brain chemistry abnormalities. Students prefer to meet their own needs through legitimate self-expression and assertion. They revert to misbehavior only when they think that the more socially appropriate win–win avenues for need-meeting are likely to be unprofitable, blocked, too difficult to attempt, or unsafe to try.

Much like a person trying to obtain a candy bar from a vending machine, the student inserts a coin of assertion and hopes to receive a helpful response from the environment at home, in the community, or at school. When the proverbial candy bar doesn't emerge, the student kicks the machine of life because ordinary assertion didn't result in the expected fulfillment and meeting of needs.

Almost all misbehavior is also a search for power. Misbehavior starts from a feeling of being one-down, discouraged, vulnerable, treated unfairly, in doubt, or violated in some way. Because it is an attempt to feel power and strength, misbehavior has a certain firmness and resilience to it. It has a certain drive. Albeit an unwise choice, considering the likely distortions in perception of self and others, misbehavior may seem to be the student's best option. It is, however, always basically a mistake. A wiser course of action would be to seek power through cooperative efforts in an atmosphere of mutual respect with the expectation that a win–win result will occur.

Sometimes misbehavior is a legitimate self-expression in an emotionally unhealthy situation—a good choice in a bad circumstance.

Almost all misbehavior is also a search for power.

The student who runs away from an abusive parent is a case in point. Another common occurrence is acting-out as a surrogate for some other member of the family. The student who witnesses his/her mother being repeatedly brutalized by his/her father, for example, may attack the father or run away from home. Yet these fight-or-flight behavioral choices should rightfully be made by the student's mother, whose under-assertion begs for rescue. The student is acting-out a family pathology scenario. In this sense, the student acts as the mother's proxy for escape from an emotionally overwhelming circumstance.

The key to breaking a cycle of misbehavior is to crack the code of its hidden goals and purposes. Misbehavior is usually a detour taken because a more direct route to meeting personal needs is blocked. When the adult doesn't respond in a fulfilling way to the student's appeal for needed services (safety, love, or interaction, for example), one way to force a response is to misbehave. In this sense, misbehavior points to and reflects the student's unmet needs.

Get below the surface of the student's antics. What appears to be simple contrariness, laziness, or bad attitude is better understood as a reflection of some serious, unmet needs. Misbehaviors don't involve a need to not study, but they could involve a need to not feel stupid, not feel incompetent, or even not be bossed by an authority figure. Imagine that every misbehaving or malfunctioning student is wearing a sign that says "Help me better meet my needs."

Using judgmental terms doesn't create much progress. Branding students as *lazy* and *goof-offs* won't guide you in a helpful direction. Teachers, parents, and counselors who replace judgment with empathy are most effective at reaching malfunctioning students. The student who won't turn in homework has unmet needs having to do with much more serious processes than a need to goof off.

Interpret misbehavior and malfunctioning by uncovering unrecognized needs the student has. Misbehavior is somewhat of a compass. It points to and reflects the underlying needfulness. Notice carefully the actions of the student and the involved adults, as well as the emotional responses the student tends to elicit from involved adults.

Five Types Of Needs

Five basic categories of needfulness underlie the misbehavior and malfunctioning of students. If one of the links in a five-link chain is broken, the chain can no longer support a heavy weight. In the same way, if any of the five basic needs is not consistently met, the student will malfunction or misbehave. Giving students these five categories of supportive messages on a daily basis should be a prime objective for every teacher, counselor, and parent. A child or teen who fails to regularly receive strong support from these five aspects is at great risk for malfunctioning or misbehaving. The strong, simultaneous sense of these five needs being met can be referred to as *encouragement.* Absence of a strong sense of all five awarenesses is *discouragement.* Misbehaving students are invariably discouraged students.

Our goal is to provide encouragement. To do so, we must communicate messages that support the student's sense of affirmation in the five areas of personal functioning. We want every student to experience a personal chain of encouragement, with all five links unbroken and strong. Each link has a name.

The First Link: Social Impact

The student feels a personal connection to parents, friends, family, classmates, neighborhood, pets, school, ethnic group, and country. These connections impart a sense of belonging and fitting in. Parents and teachers thank the student for favors he/she performs and express their delight at his/her contributions and appropriate behavior that generates positive results.

For example, the teacher could invite the entire class to make a quilt, with each student contributing a square. The teacher thanks the students for their contributions and the students feel a sense of belonging and fitting in. The honest responses of adults and peer acquaintances in the student's life provide a realistic sense of being a meaningful part of social entities—family, class, club, and neighborhood.

The student who experiences a strong sense of the first link will learn that his/her contributions matter. The student who is discouraged by an inadequately experienced sense of social impact will have far different perceptions. The student learns to believe that his/her contributions have no result and don't matter. He/she regards others as having overlooked his/her contributions or as having taken them for granted and feels rejected or disliked by peers and somewhat estranged from them.

The Second Link: Self-Direction

The student feels influential over the factors in his/her life and over his/her own destiny. He/she is given ample opportunity to express opinions, exercise personal choices, and express wants. A teacher who offers several choices for earning a grade of *A* and several for earning a *B* gives the student a

great sense of mastering his/her own fate at school. Perhaps the art teacher offers several media and artistic productions to choose from. Perhaps the school has career day, when the student can gain a sense of being able to help determine his/her own academic and vocational directions. Perhaps the counselor helps the student explore several different educational and vocational options during planning for the transition following high school graduation.

The student has a sense that his/her wants are honored and respected by the important people in his/her life. In turn, he/she is willing to show empathy and courtesy toward others as they express their needs and voice their wants. He/she develops a functioning conscience and can choose the right options, resist undesirable peer pressure, and come to believe that he/she is ultimately responsible for the choices he/she makes.

The student who is discouraged by a perceived lack of this link of the chain of encouragement has a different view. The student learns to conclude that how he/she wants to do things doesn't matter. He/she feels bossed, dominated, micromanaged, powerless, and weak. Believing that he/she is not being given enough decision-making opportunity, the student experiences an ever-expanding inner pressure to assert his/her own wants, even at the expense of others' happiness and rights. He/she is at risk for not developing a strong conscience and for being unable to resist peer pressure. He/she is likely to blame the consequences of his/her choices on external circumstances or on other people who were involved.

The Third Link: Self-Worth

The student has a sure sense of being safe, cherished, loved, respected, and deeply valued by the adults and peers in his/her life. Parents treat the child or teen with courtesy and respect. They honor and protect his/her rights and protect him/her from harm. They rescue the child or teen if he/she is hurt or his/her rights are violated, and they empathize with any agonies he/she experiences. They tuck the child in at bedtime and spend special time with him/her to show their love. The child's birthday is celebrated without giving compensatory gifts to siblings. Adults and peers seek out his/her companionship and, by their actions and words indicate that the child or teen has profound merit and infinite worth and lovability.

Misbehaving students are invariably discouraged students.

Others empathize with the student's feelings and respond with caring and concern. Teachers show a personal interest in the student and treat him/her with dignity, courtesy, and respect. The student feels like a worthwhile being in a transcendent, infinite way and feels loved, protected, and cared for. This third link involves the student learning that his/her very presence is precious and matters immensely.

A student discouraged by a lack of this link, on the other hand, feels quite the opposite. His/her presence seems to mean nothing to anybody. Parents and teachers treat him/her in a discourteous, even abusive fashion. The student feels hurt, hated, and victimized. Far from being cherished, he/she feels abandoned, double-crossed, and violated by people and by life itself. He/she feels rejected and unloved and has no desire to respond to such treatment with kindness.

The student feels a strong need to gather any evidence that he/she is noticed or appreciated in any way, and an even stronger need to protect him/herself from further harm and degradation. He/she experiences a constant inner pressure to stay safe from being hurt any more.

The Fourth Link: Self-Confidence

The student feels capable, competent, and talented. Parents, teachers, and counselors show faith in his/her abilities. What they ask is geared to the student's readiness level, so that he/she experiences an *I can do it* attitude resulting from daily accomplishments at home and at school.

The teacher avoids overwhelming the student with assignments beyond his/her level, and also avoids boring him/her with insultingly easy assignments. Because counselors, teachers, and parents have a permissive attitude toward any errors the student makes, he/she isn't hampered by perfectionism. He/she develops a robust feeling of personal competence and a willingness to try hard despite the possibility of making a few errors.

This fourth link involves the student learning that his/her efforts matter and are acknowledged, appreciated, and supported by the authority figures in his/her life. The student becomes self-confident in a healthy, humble way. He/she is accepting of his/her limitations and recognizes when he/she needs help. The student is not arrogant, grandiose, or selfish.

A student who is discouraged by a lack of these encouraging messages learns to believe that his/her efforts don't count for much. When the student makes errors, parents and teachers scold him/her for not trying hard enough. They compare the student's performance with that of his/her siblings or classmates and criticize and punish him/her for making mistakes.

If assignments are too difficult, the student may conclude that he/she is stupid. If they are too easy, the student may conclude that the teacher regards him/her as stupid and that school is "dumb and boring." Intimidated by the notion of making any mistakes, the student shrinks from attempting a task that looks challenging. He/she experiences an inner pressure to escape from adults' intimidating performance expectations.

The Fifth Link: Stimulation

Excited about what happens at school, the student explores the nooks and crannies of the subject matter the teacher is sharing, asks questions, volunteers answers in class discussion, and has no difficulty staying focused on the content the teacher is presenting. The student finds the world a fascinating place and welcomes opportunities to learn about it and about life.

Rather than waiting for the teacher to be entertaining, the student finds meaning and relevance in the material or manufactures relevance by mentally jazzing it up and creating acronyms to memorize information for an upcoming test. This fifth link involves the student learning that his/her alertness matters. He/she devotes energy to maintaining alertness in class, regardless of how inherently interesting or uninteresting the lesson may be.

The student who lacks a sense of stimulation is likely to be bored with school, with little energy for doing more than the minimum necessary to pass the course. Alertness doesn't matter to this student, who has little interest in contributing to class discussion. His/her priorities are likely to be topsy-turvy, with considerable concern allocated to frivolous matters, gossip, and the latest computer games.

This student considers the content of classroom instruction to be utterly boring and dumb and blames the teacher for not being sufficiently entertaining to arouse his/her alertness. He/she feels uncomfortable adult pressure to attend class, participate in class discussion, perform seatwork and homework assignments, and pass tests. The student also experiences a constant inner pressure to create stimulating events.

Why Anger Is Often Involved

Emotional hurt and consequent anger are often at the core of misbehavior. Anger is an energizing, focusing, emotional defensive response to a perceived primary hurt or stress. It readies the student for *opposing* in a way that decreases or eliminates the stressor, or *removing* him/herself from the stressful situation.

Anger provides two elements to facilitate its defensive function: a burst of extra energy and a narrowing of focus or intent. The diagnostician's role is to assess the stressors and the student's coping mechanisms. Counselors, teachers, supervisors, and parents may help the student use anger more effectively by transforming it into constructive striving, determination, and assertion directed toward more-effective meeting of the student's needs.

A student who perceives a stressor may counterattack with the anger-induced narrowing of focus and an energy burst. A student who perceives a stressor to be inaccessible may select a substitute target. One example of this response is the student who responds to parents' emotional and verbal abuse by bullying other children.

The Mishandling And Handling Of Anger

The four most common ways children and teens mishandle their anger can be symbolized by the acronym *RUDE*:

- **R** — **REPEATED** useless venting, as in pounding a pillow
- **U** — **UNDER-EXPRESSING** anger and keeping it inside, as in depression
- **D** — **DUMPING** and outwardly misdirecting anger, as in bullying
- **E** — **EXAGGERATING** anger expression, as in having tantrums

Ideally, anger should:

- be expressed rather than hidden
- result in stress reduction or in the student's removal from the threatening situation
- be sufficiently intense to accomplish its legitimate social purpose without being overdone
- result in confronting the source stressor rather than substitute targets

Biochemical Imbalances

Other causes of anger are biochemical imbalances or other faulty processes in the brain or central nervous system function. Disturbances in social perception and behavior control such as psychotic disorders or the aftermath of brain injury and chronic conditions such as ADHD and bipolar disorder can trigger misbehavior. An emotional and socially related overlay often draws the attention of helping professionals. Before proceeding with psychological solutions, it is important to clarify the underlying role of any relevant physiological abnormalities.

Why Sibling Rivalry Can Be An Issue

Widely, though mistakenly, considered unavoidable, sibling rivalry won't be a significant factor unless it becomes excessive. Siblings who perceive that sufficient love is available within the family experience minimal rivalry.

Perception of insufficient love can lead to such family stress indicators as:

- *angel-brat* roles in children
- self-perpetuating struggles for revenge
- bullying
- jealousy
- reciprocal violation of boundaries and living space
- stealing
- a lack of affirming dialogue between siblings

The most frequent comparisons among severely competitive siblings involve:

- physical attractiveness
- intellectual and academic productivity
- athletic and physical abilities
- cleanliness
- tendency to act in responsible ways
- personal interests
- possession of talents

Whenever one child commands an inordinate amount of parents' time and energy, his/her siblings' total parental contact diminishes. Chronic disease, ADHD, sensory processing disorder, or chronic misbehavior in one child, for example, can perpetuate such circumstances and lead to intense sibling rivalry.

Abnormal parental focusing on one child because of a parent's emotional difficulties or difficulties within the parents' relationship can become a catalyst for pathological sibling rivalry. A mother may pamper and overindulge a sickly, clumsy, or unathletic son whose father continuously rejects him. Siblings who resent their mother's shifting of attention away from them may act-out against the pampered, rejected son.

Siblings who perceive that sufficient love is available within the family experience minimal rivalry.

Family Constellation And Sibling Rivalry

Sibling issues can magnify family constellation factors. Sibling rivalry polarizes roles and characteristics of positions within the family. Traits usually associated with an oldest sibling, for example, are likely to be somewhat exaggerated in the oldest child in a family with intense sibling rivalry. Families with little sibling rivalry, on the other hand, tend to produce children who possess only some of the traits typically associated with being the first, middle, and youngest children in the family.

CHAPTER 2

Gather Data From All Relevant Sources

When exploring a student's emotional and behavioral difficulties, use as many sources of information as possible. You can:

- obtain tests
- use structured interviewing procedures
- talk with siblings and parents
- confer with teachers
- review school records
- obtain a medical history

Record your observations before and during your interview of the student. Include information generated from your interaction with the student. Your emotional responses are an indication that the student may be eliciting similar responses from other adults.

Misbehavior Has Many Causes

Assess misbehavior in as broad a context as possible, and don't narrow your focus early in the diagnostic process. Assume that the misbehavior has many causes and serves many purposes for the student. Contrast differences and inconsistencies you uncover from various sources of information. Track down reasons for differing accounts of the student's behavior. There will often be distortion in others' perceptions of the student and the misbehavior. Conduct that one teacher perceives as *conviction* may indicate *obstinance* to another. Your task is to understand the reality, unclouded by others' misperceptions and biases.

If history indicates that the student has been developmentally delayed or slow in passing ordinary milestones, identify those areas in which the student functions below the norm. Refer to reliable charts and tables to gain a working knowledge of expected growth and development guidelines as well as typical academic and social skills at different age levels.

Accept the student's statements as probably truthful, but contrast them with your observations and feelings during the interview. Children and teens don't always tell the truth to authority figures who interview them! Nor are they usually aware of why they choose courses of action that result in misbehavior.

Positives And Strengths

Hunt for positives and strengths as well as for negatives. Note such evidence of respect and tolerance as taking turns, not disturbing others while working, and waiting quietly while other students complete assignments; such evidence of courage as taking reasonable risks and remaining calm under pressure; and such evidence of encouragement as an optimistic attitude and focusing on the positive aspects of a situation.

Family Interaction Information

Plan to obtain information about family interaction, including strengths and assets available to the student within the family. Gather information on any medical condition or neurological difficulties that might affect brain function, sensory awareness, perception, memory, focusing, fidgeting, or muscle performance. Discover positive and negative aspects of the student's self-concept, and strive for a well-substantiated conclusion about the student's goals and purposes of misbehaving.

School-Centered Information

Obtain additional, school-centered information focusing on such areas as the student's abilities at play, problem-solving skills, speech and language functions, and academic performance.

Assess Behavior In Different Settings

The universal principles of encouragement tend to apply to all age groups and a wide range of relationships. Responses of such authority figures as childcare supervisors, baby sitters, school administrators, and teachers often parallel those of parents.

Discouraged children will usually try to manipulate most authority figures in the same way.

Discouraged children's underlying needs remain the same; the cast of characters upon whom they act-out their needfulness varies from setting to setting. If the opportunity presents itself, interview parents, grandparents, student-care providers, and others who supervise the student for extended periods.

Assess External Stressors

Worry adds to family stress and can ultimately contribute to misbehavior. Common external stressors include:

- parents' extended work schedules
- inadequate living space in the home
- inadequate access to safe and suitable play areas near the home
- chronic health condition(s) of a family member or members
- parental psychiatric dysfunction

A family that frequently moves or changes income sources faces a host of stresses.

Ask about financial problems, the total debt load the parents are carrying, and opportunities for the family to improve its financial outlook. Distribution of allowances is worth asking about, because money is a resource the student can use to meet his/her needs and thereby alleviate some stresses that can lead to misbehavior.

Assess Physiological Impairments

A malfunctioning brain can contribute to misbehavior. Ask parents for an overview of the student's medical history. It might be beneficial to obtain medical records from the student's physician.

Approximately 7% of children and teens in the United States have ADHD, the majority being boys.

Ask about the student's dietary habits. About 40% of nutrition and calories should come at breakfast. Children and teens need balanced diets in order to maintain:

- physical health
- emotional resilience
- self-control
- sufficient energy to cope with demands encountered at school
- reserve energy for vigorous activity

Teenage girls need extra iron. Nutritionists continue to debate the relationship between food consumption and children's and teens' behavior. The connection varies greatly from one student to the next, and misbehavior is the result of several converging factors.

A diet that includes a meager breakfast or no breakfast at all is less effective at preventing misbehavior than a nutritious breakfast. The same could be said about lunch and the evening meal. A diet that emphasizes starch and sugary foods and includes only small amounts of protein, vitamins, minerals, and fatty acids is highly suspect.

ADHD, which affects performance and behavior at school, is one of the most common results of physiological imbalance. Approximately 7% of children and teens in the United States have ADHD, the majority being boys. It is often helpful to screen for the probability of ADHD. *The Taylor Hyperactivity Screening Checklist* (see page 27) is useful for this purpose, at least to screen for the hyperactivity component present in the majority of students with ADHD. The score is the total number of items in Column B plus twice the number of items in Column C. If the child's score is:

- **0 to 24:** clinically impaired hyperactivity is not indicated
- **25 to 27:** borderline
- **28 to 32:** mild hyperactivity
- **33 to 37:** moderate hyperactivity
- **38 to 42:** severe hyperactivity

Diagnosing ADHD is a complicated affair, as no existing medical tests definitively rule it in or out. The most valid indicator is a thorough behavioral history combined with observation of the student. Diagnosticians should also hunt for the various difficulties in family relationships that often accompany ADHD.

THE TAYLOR HYPERACTIVITY SCREENING CHECKLIST

For each of the 21 behaviors listed below, put an X in one of the three boxes to show what is typical for the child. Rate the child's behavior when not being supervised, helped, or reminded; when not watching television or a computer screen; and when not receiving any kind of diet or medication to control behavior.

Indicate the trend. Try to avoid column B ratings. A 51% trend in either direction should merit an A or C rating. Compared with other children of approximately the same age, this child typically shows behavior:

A MORE LIKE THIS — **B NO TREND** — **C MORE LIKE THIS**

A		B		C
	Quiet person		Noisy and talkative person	
	Voice volume is soft or average		Voice is generally too loud for the situation	
	Few mouth or body noises		Makes lots of clicks, whistles, and sounds with mouth or body	
	Walks at appropriate times		Flits around, runs ahead, needs to be called back, jumpy	
	Keeps hands to self		Pokes, touches, feels, and grabs	
	Appears calm, can be still		Often has a body part moving; fidgets with hands or feet; squirmy	
	Can just sit		Must be doing something to occupy self when sitting; quickly bored	
	Contemplative, deliberate, not impulsive		Too quick to react, impulsive, engages mouth and muscles before brain	
	Understands why parents/teacher/others are displeased after misbehavior		Feels picked on, is surprised and confused about why others are displeased; doesn't connect own actions with others' reactions	
	Plans and thinks ahead to consequences before acting; careful		Does things without considering the consequences ahead of time; doesn't plan well; careless	
	Concerned about punishments and consequences; submissive		Pretends to have an *I don't care* attitude if threatened or punished; defiant	
	Avoids other children's mischief		Attracted or curious about mischief; gets involved or starts it	
	Obeys directions and follows orders		Disobeys or forgets; needs supervision or reminding	
	Constant mood with mild or slow mood changes; a calm person		Moody, unpredictable, quick to anger or cry	
	Easygoing, handles frustration without much anger, patient, can be teased		Irritable, impatient, easily frustrated	
	Emotions are reasonably controlled, are not extreme, and don't disrupt relationships		Emotions are extreme and poorly controlled; no *damper pedal* on emotions; explosive; tantrums	
	Cooperates with, obeys and enforces the rules of work and play		Argues and gripes about the rules; wants to be the exception; oppositional	
	Gives up when denied a requested privilege, item, or activity		Badgers, pesters, pushes, won't give up or take *no* for an answer	
	Concentrates and blocks out distractions when working on something of medium interest, or when mental discipline is required		Easily distracted by noises and people nearby; short attention span	
	Follows through; has an organized approach to activities; finishes projects		Flits from activity to activity; starts things without finishing them; gets sidetracked	
	Doesn't try to bother or hurt others with words		Needles, teases, "mouthy;" has to have the last word	

Map The Family Constellation

Obtain from the outset a clear understanding of the family constellation. Note ages of all family members. Find out about adoptions, previous families for each parent, and other factors involved with the creation of this current family unit. A good way to depict the family constellation is to write the first name of each family member inside a separate circle. Starting with the oldest child, write beneath each circle the number of years separating the oldest child's birth from the birth of the children whose names are written in other circles.

This counselor's notations indicate that Bruce (age 39) and Ellen (age 37) have been married for 8 years. This is Bruce's second marriage and Ellen's third marriage. Bruce's daughter from one of his previous marriages is Amy (age 13), and Ellen's adopted son from a previous marriage is Josh, who is 4 years younger than Amy (age 9). Jake (age 6) was born to this couple.

Listing ages of the parents and oldest child serves as a reference point for how old family members were when first interviewed. The ages will advance in subsequent years, but the relative ages will remain the same. Josh will always be four years younger than Amy, and Jake will always be seven years younger than Amy.

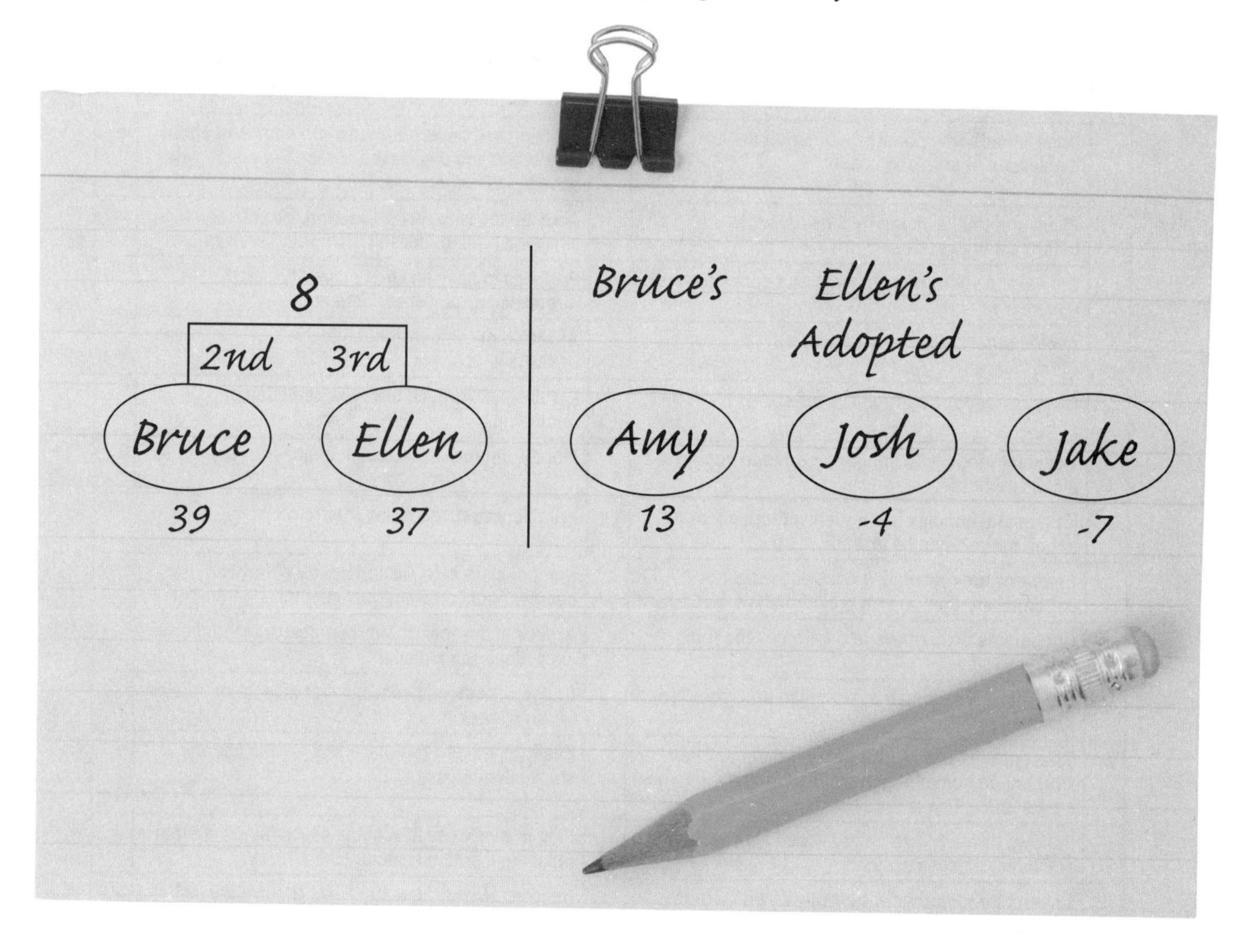

Gather Information From Parents

You may have a chance to interview or observe the student's parents. Their responses to his/her problematic behavior might be similar to those of teachers, because all the involved adults are in positions to lead, guide, discipline, challenge, and supervise the student. They are also in positions to become targets for the student's manipulations.

It is not unusual that a student who gets into power struggles with teachers also manipulates parents into senseless arguments and showdowns of defiance. Ask whether parents experience the types of emotional and behavioral responses displayed to the teachers. The home environment is sometimes a training ground in which the student develops and refines various strategies for evoking predictable responses from classmates and teachers.

Some parents, on the other hand, report no such responses on their part and claim a more harmonious atmosphere at home than has been reported at school. If the parents are accurate, you have evidence that the core conflict has to do with such issues as the classroom atmosphere created by an individual teacher. The central issue would then be more situationally based and less a reflection of emotional problems in the student.

Key items to ask parents about are indicated in the *Parent Interview Checklist* (page 30).

Interviewing both parents together allows you to observe their style of interaction and detect relationship nuances that might otherwise go unnoticed. Contrasting styles of dealing with specific issues, such as moments of the student's misbehavior, are more likely to become evident if you interview both parents together than if you interview each parent separately.

Parents' contributions to their children's eventual misbehavior have to do with increasing the stresses with which the children must cope. Common parenting risk factors to assess are:

- insufficient modeling and guidance
- an excessively harsh and punitive disciplinary approach
- child abuse
- an inadequate stress umbrella
- child neglect
- over-involvement with the student

PARENT INTERVIEW CHECKLIST

- ☐ Social history of the family, including past marriages and step-parenting situations
- ☐ Medical, developmental, and psychiatric history
- ☐ Major current and past stresses impinging on the family
- ☐ The nature and quality of the relationship between the parents and involved step-parents, including non-custodial parents
- ☐ Self-concept
- ☐ Sibling relationships
- ☐ Past and current concerns expressed by school personnel about the student
- ☐ Parents' wants and expectations about the help you are offering
- ☐ Strengths and weaknesses in each parent's relationship with the student
- ☐ Parents' past and current theories about the student's problem behaviors
- ☐ Concerns about the student, expressed as anything the parents regard as unusual and problematic

Hunt For Parental Over-Involvement

Often driven by a parent's guilt feelings, over-involvement reflects too great an infiltration into the child's arena of life. Concern for the child's difficulties may tempt the parent to run interference in many settings. The result can be disastrous. The parent can become overworked and physically and emotionally exhausted, while the child becomes increasingly demanding toward the parent and inept at handling the challenges of life.

Over-involvement also sabotages self-esteem, as the child gradually becomes convinced that a high degree of parental involvement is always necessary. Children start out thinking that parents are always right. So if a parent thinks all this extra service is needed, the child concludes that it must indeed be needed. Watch for the following common types of parental over-involvement.

Overprotection

The parent excessively shields the student from potential dangers in non-skill-related activities. Constantly fearful that something bad or overwhelming might happen to the child, the parent feels a need to intervene so that no misfortunes occur.

The parent may develop what looks like a reflexive, almost unthinking defensive response. Shielding a child from any potentially difficult situation, the overprotective parent robs him/her of opportunities for growth and challenge. The parent's motto is, "Don't do it, because bad things might happen." Gradually becoming convinced that nearly every situation is full of danger and defeat, the child learns to feel that he/she is unable to cope with stress. Eventually, the child may shrink from almost any situation that involves unknowns, risks, or challenges. The child's self-confidence becomes a prisoner of the parent's fearfulness.

Over-Nurturing

The overprotective parent often lavishes nurture onto the child, who doesn't learn to cope as an independent being. The child remains ignorant and dependent on the parent, who is delighted to bestow an expanding array of services on the increasingly helpless child. Gradually, the child fails to learn how to function independently in such skill-related self-care areas as cooking, dressing, doing homework, arising in the morning, getting to bed at night, and bathing.

Spoiling

The overindulgent parent attempts to shield the child from every frustration. The parent bestows extra attention, service, food, or material goods and ends up doing things that the child should do. A child patronized in this fashion becomes increasingly demanding and may attempt to increase the parent's underlying feelings of guilt, as if he/she is entitled to excessive service and material goodies.

Pitying

Pity is a discouraging, misdirected, and overstated attempt at sympathy. It conveys the parent's doubt about the child's ability to cope. It is a failed attempt to empathize with the child's experiences of frustration, hurt, or difficulty.

Parental pity exaggerates the child's misfortunes. The pitying parent may also feel guilty for not having sufficiently protected or indulged the child. The child's misfortunes may remind the pitying parent of self-assumed responsibilities for having worsened the child's problems. Motivated by a combination of personal guilt and pity, the parent may make exceptions that allow the child to avoid such ordinary challenges as performing chores, participating at school, doing homework, and assuming responsibilities.

Mutual Dependence

The excessive closeness that develops when family members experience such long-term stresses as disease or a deteriorating marriage can tempt a child or teen to try to meet a parent's emotional needs. Or it can tempt a parent to entice a child or teen to meet emotional needs that should be met by another adult.

The parent might become a teen's best friend and try to meet too many social needs better met through interaction with other teens. The resulting parent-teen bond is too tight. Mutual dependence severely restricts the teen's social and emotional development, and shouldering adult-level stresses renders him/her very susceptible to emotional overburdening.

Nagging

Probably the most common form of parental over-involvement, nagging consists of piling up reminder messages in piggyback fashion, one seemingly stacked upon another. The parent issues an intermittent stream of directives, suggestions, commands, criticism, coaxing, or threats.

To the child or teen, the frequency of these piggybacked messages dilutes their importance. A cycle can develop in which the parent feels an obligation to nag because of the apparent need for more reminders. Yet the more the parent nags, the more sloppy, slow, or forgetful the child or teen seems to become. The parent feels increasingly pressured into nagging and reminding. The child may come to view the parent's nagging as a form of attention, and a *Misbehavior–Nag Cycle* develops.

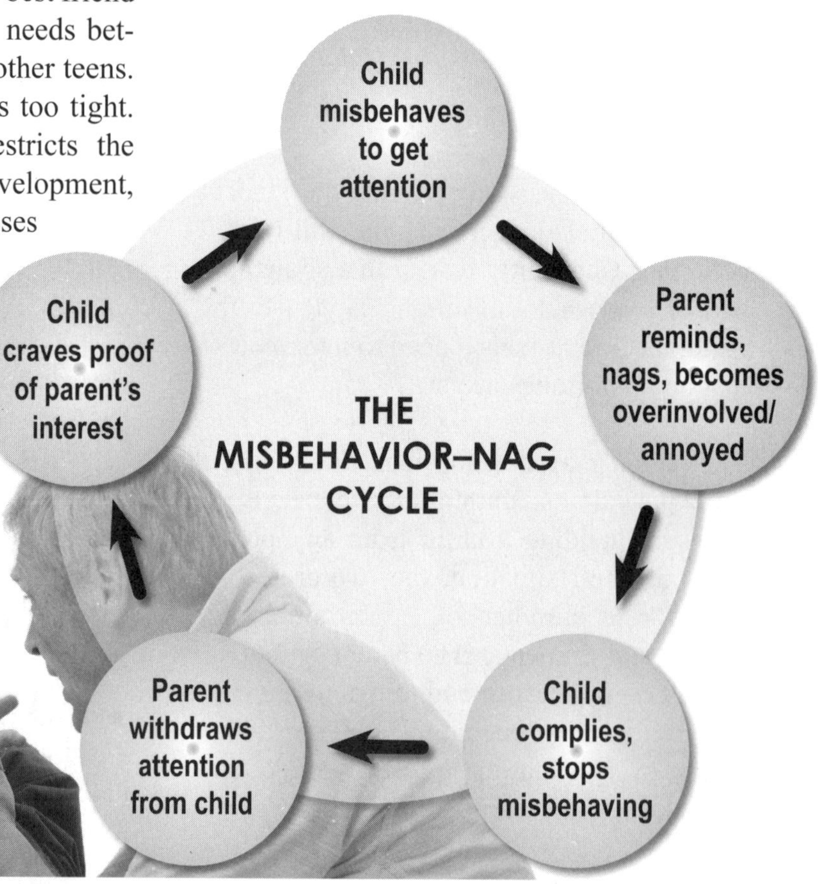

Find The Family's Conflict Hot Spots

To uncover pathological patterns of parent-child relationships, describe what you suspect might be happening. Then ask the parent to comment on how accurate your hypothesis is. Identify the hardest time of a typical day for the parent, in terms of interacting with the child or teen. The greatest conflicts usually occur around such daily routines as arising in the morning, getting ready for the day, doing chores, sibling interactions, mealtimes, and bedtimes.

C And D Percent

One of the best measures to obtain is the total amount of nagging, reminding, scolding, punishing, and criticizing that the parents are doing. The simplest measure is the *C and D (Correction and Direction) Percent.* Suppose Mark is the misbehaving student. Ask the parent:

> *"Of all the messages you give Mark, what percentage involves correction (C) scolding, criticizing, reprimanding, punishing, using a harsh tone, telling him what he did wrong and/or direction (D) nagging, reminding, ordering, telling him what to do? Of all the messages you give Mark, what percentage is corrective or directive in nature?"*

Very stressed parent-child relationships usually have C and D figures above 60%. The ideal is about 25%.

Repeating A Command

Another important measure is the average number of times the parent typically repeats a command or request to the student. In very stressed parent-student relationships, this figure is more than *three.* Ask:

> *"On the average, how many times do you repeat yourself before Mark does what you want or request?"*

Raising One's Voice

Another important measure is the number of times a day that parents raise their voices toward the child or teen. The ideal answer is *zero.*

Assess Parent–Child Bonding

To assess some of the bases for building a stronger parent-child bond, determine the frequency and quality of *pairing moments.* Ask:

> *"How often do you and Mark do something recreational alone together for at least 15 minutes?"*

The ideal is at least *once per week.* These pairing times can include bedtime tuck-ins, lunch, or virtually any companionship moment of a positive nature. There should be opportunity for direct interaction that affirms the parent's love and allows the child or teen to experience undiluted parental attention. A useful guideline is that one high-quality 15-minute period of togetherness each week is enough to assure the child or teen of his/her importance and worth to the parent. In very stressed families, the frequency and quality of pairing activities are almost always very low or nonexistent, or there is a great discrepancy in how loved the child or teen feels after experiencing these moments with one parent or the other.

Identify Stress Patterns Between Parents

A child's problematic behavior can create stress in parents' relationships with one another. Each parent must adjust to the other's response to the child. The parents must also handle the responsibilities of leading the family, including a host of stresses stemming from interrelationships among family members. If one parent has a severe emotional problem or a profound abnormality such as alcoholism, drug abuse, or criminal behavior, the ripple effects can threaten the social, emotional, and physical well-being of all family members.

The following maladaptive parenting patterns tend to occur in families with chronically misbehaving or malfunctioning children or teens. Many of these patterns emerge so gradually that the parents are slow to recognize their development. Use the *Parental Stress Pattern Checklist* (page 39) to record the maladaptive parenting patterns revealed in your interviews.

Partial Denial

One spouse denies that misbehavior or malfunctioning occurs; the other recognizes its existence within the family. The denying parent criticizes the non-denying one as being overprotective or too emotional. The denying parent minimizes the problems the child and family are experiencing and might dismiss the problem as a phase, as ordinary rough-and-tumble activity, as merely a personality quirk, as an indication that "boys will be boys," or as necessary preparation for the cold, cruel world.

Joint Denial

Both parents deny any need for professional involvement. This pattern is particularly destructive because the misbehavior almost always gradually worsens, shielded by the protective bubble of parental denial. Never realizing what they are dealing with, the parents remain ill-equipped to stop the misbehavior.

Partial Abuse

Seething with anger toward the child for misbehaving, for embarrassing the family, or for drawing professional attention, one parent commits one or more of the five types of abuse: physical, emotional, verbal, sexual, or ritual. The non-abusive parent might not join in the abuse, but might provide illicit support. Perhaps the non-abusive parent uses whitewash techniques like becoming over-involved and assuming all parenting duties, or attempts to protect the child by keeping knowledge of misbehavior from the abusing parent. But the non-abusive parent doesn't stop the ongoing abuse from occurring.

Joint Abuse

Both parents participate in one or more of the five forms of abuse. Couples who commit such abuse manage to justify their actions. When the abuse comes to the attention of authorities, the family often moves out of the area and the parents continue their abuse. Sometimes a cycle develops (see below) in which the parents, ashamed and embarrassed by the child's poor functioning or chronic misbehavior, abuse the child. This results in increased acting-out by the increasingly violated and embittered child.

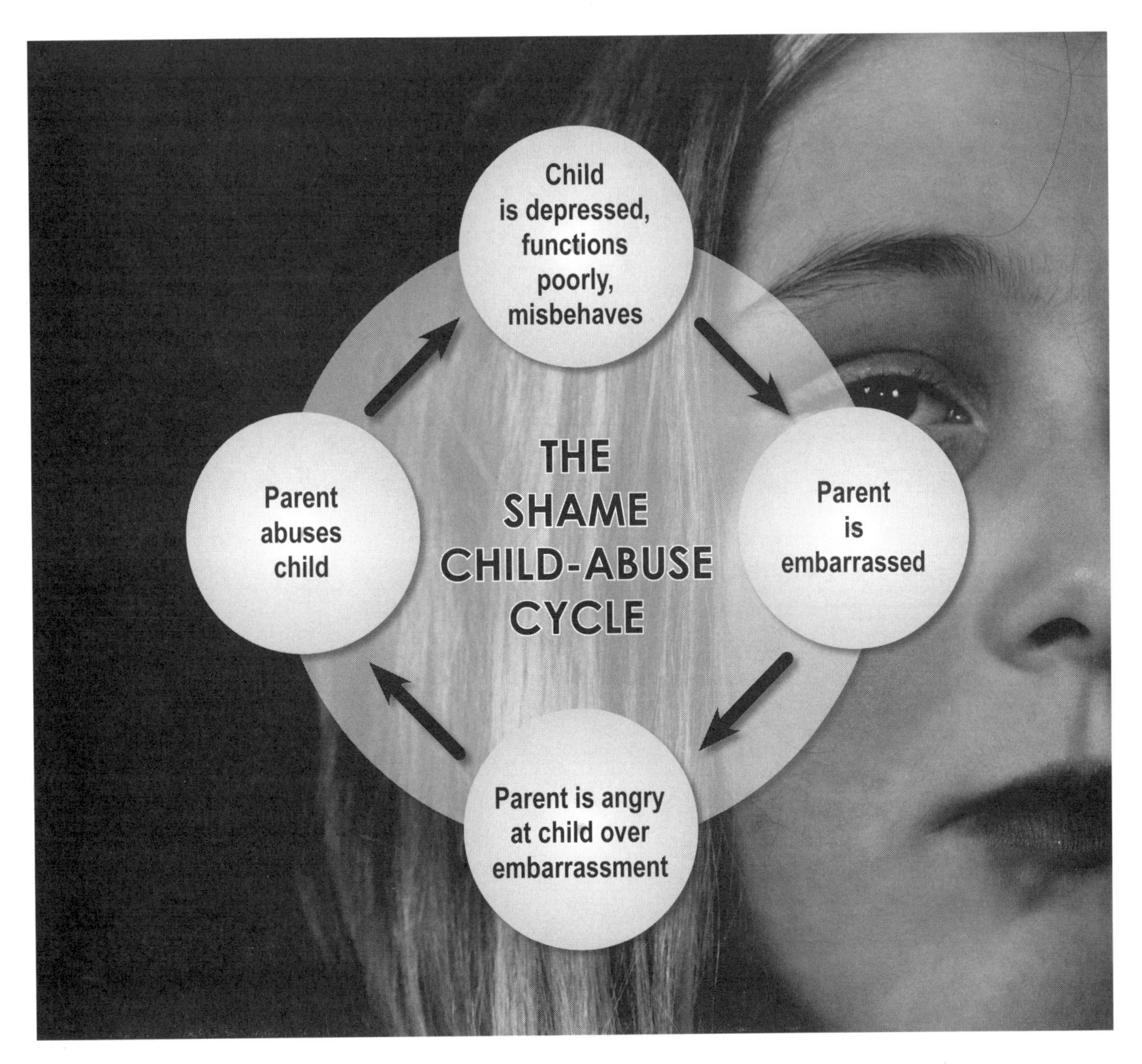

Partial Over-Involvement

One parent becomes over-involved with the child in any of the several forms discussed earlier. The other parent might respond in any of a variety of ways, including over-compensating in the opposite direction and becoming abusive toward the child.

Joint Over-Involvement

Both parents become over-involved and deal with the child in a servant-like way, taking on responsibility for aspects of life that the child should be managing independently. The result is a demanding child, unprepared to meet the challenges of life, catered to by two exhausted and guilt-ridden parents.

Somctimes a cycle develops in which the parents begin to resent the huge drain on their time and energy brought about by their over-involvement. They then feel guilty for feeling angry toward the child, and attempt to atone by finding even more ways to over-serve the child.

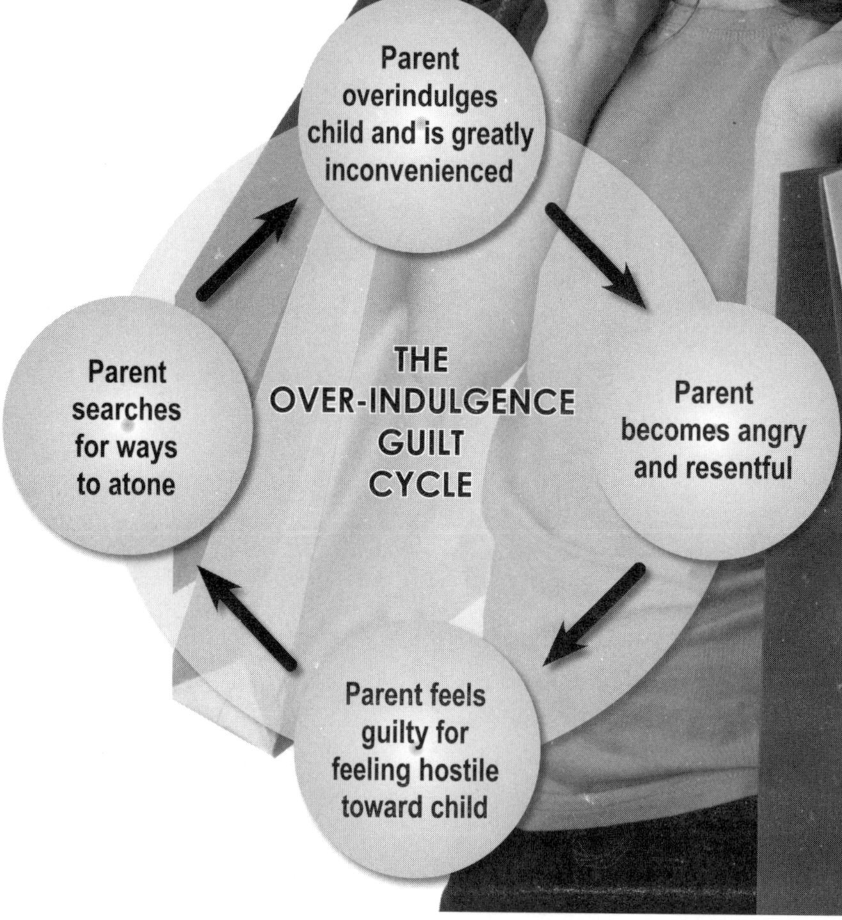

THE OVER-INDULGENCE GUILT CYCLE

Parent overindulges child and is greatly inconvenienced

Parent becomes angry and resentful

Parent feels guilty for feeling hostile toward child

Parent searches for ways to atone

Partial Emotional Bankruptcy

One parent declares emotional bankruptcy, forcing the other parent to assume total responsibility for managing the child. The bankrupt parent typically becomes neglectful and acts irresponsibly about many aspects of parenting and family leadership. The parent who is left with the majority of the burden usually becomes angry at the bankrupt parent. A cycle of self-abuse (see below), such as through alcohol or drugs, sometimes develops in the bankrupt parent.

Joint Emotional Bankruptcy

The second parent joins the first in an attempt to unload onto an external source much of the responsibility for raising the child and solving the associated problems. If the child remains in their custody, the risk for physical or emotional neglect is great. Though the parents may obtain guidance, they don't follow through on the necessary measures to structure the child's life and stop the misbehavior or the malfunctioning. The parents also usually participate in some form of self-abuse or self-destructive activity.

One-Up

One parent tries unsuccessfully to deal with problems created by the child's misbehavior or malfunctioning. The second parent seems not to understand the difficulties involved and, by criticizing the first parent, finds a way to feel superior. The first parent feels misunderstood and unfairly blamed. Both parents allow most of the responsibility for resolving the problems surrounding the child to remain with the first parent, who suffers not only from the persistent attacks by the second parent but also from the crushing burden of single-handedly managing the disruptive child.

As the misbehavior or malfunctioning gradually worsens, the first parent is blamed for not resolving things. The second parent maintains an artificial superiority by labeling the first parent *inept* or *weak*. The motive is to escape scrutiny by keeping the spotlight on the first parent's supposed shortcomings while the second parent undermines any improvements engineered by the first parent.

Mutual One-Up

When the first parent counterattacks, the two can't agree about managing the child. They struggle instead for status, each wanting to feel superior to the other. Each tries to blame the other for the child's continuing problematic behavior. Each considers the other weak, incompetent, abusive, or unfit to manage the child. Each asserts that everything would be all right if the other parent would improve.

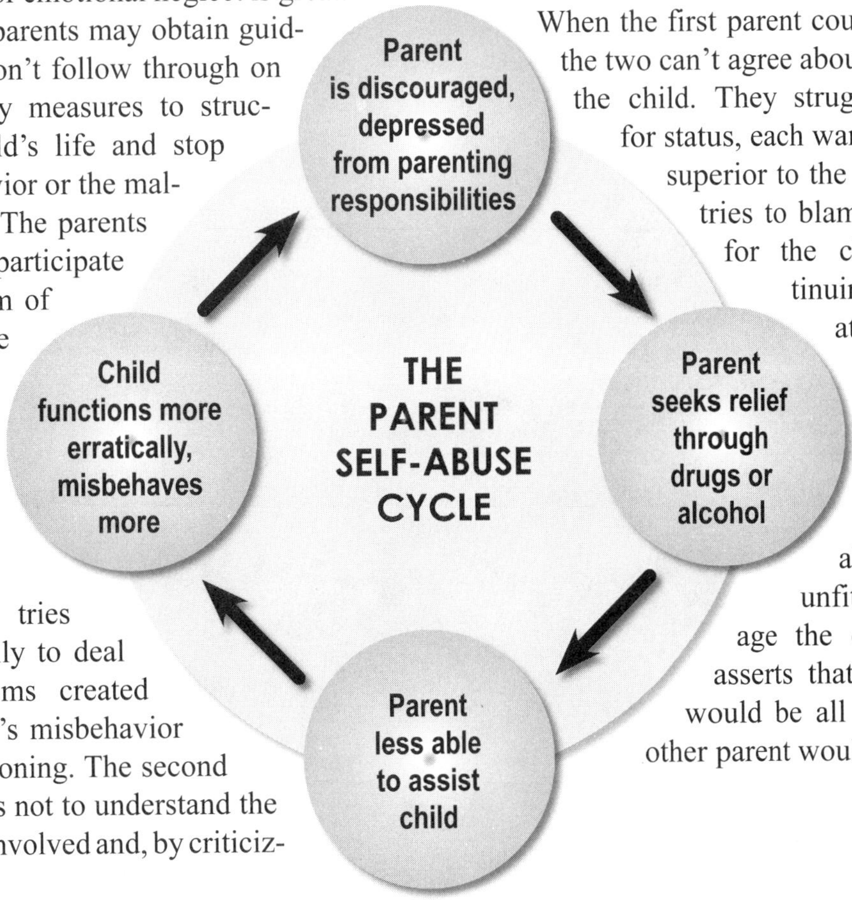

THE PARENT SELF-ABUSE CYCLE

Parent is discouraged, depressed from parenting responsibilities

Parent seeks relief through drugs or alcohol

Parent less able to assist child

Child functions more erratically, misbehaves more

Divided And Conquered

Primarily through lack of communication with each other, parents can be deceived by the child's manipulations. The situation can deteriorate so that the child eventually succeeds in dealing with only one parent rather than both. The child thus first divides, then conquers the parents. The child might, for example, learn to play one parent against the other by lying. After receiving a noncommittal answer from one parent, the child may tell the other that the first parent has given permission for a certain privilege or questionable activity that the child requested. Or the child may pester until the less-resistant parent gives in.

The child's manipulation may take advantage of an existing conflict. If the parents can't agree on whether to grant a certain privilege, the child approaches only the more-permissive parent about the matter.

Overcompensation

One parent responds to an excessive trait in the other by overdeveloping the opposite tendency. Instead of being pulled together by the child's problems, the parents drive themselves further apart. The more permissive parent may become increasingly permissive while the more restrictive parent becomes increasingly restrictive. After any specific act of misbehavior, the child is treated either too harshly or too leniently.

Probe for the occurrence of these destructive patterns. After interviewing one parent on a topic, ask the other parent's views on the same topic. Hunt for inconsistencies as well as agreements between the parents. When you uncover an inconsistency, probe further. If you suspect a pattern of overcompensation, for example, ask a question such as:

"Who's the softie?"

PARENTAL STRESS-PATTERN CHECKLIST

This checklist provides a convenient listing of factors to include when assessing the family.

- ☐ mother
- ☐ father
- ☐ denial of severity of behavior
- ☐ denial of need for intervention
- ☐ verbal abuse or near-abuse
- ☐ physical abuse or near-abuse
- ☐ emotional abuse or near-abuse
- ☐ sexual abuse or near-abuse
- ☐ ritual abuse or near-abuse
- ☐ over-protection
- ☐ over-nurturing
- ☐ spoiling
- ☐ pitying
- ☐ mutual dependence
- ☐ father's C & D % as judged by father
- ☐ father's C & D % as judged by mother
- ☐ mother's C & D % as judged by father
- ☐ mother's C & D % as judged by mother
- ☐ parent-child bonding times frequency
- ☐ parent-child bonding times typical activities
- ☐ inconsistencies noted

CHAPTER 3

Understanding & Counseling
The Misbehaving Student

How To Interview The Student

The key principles and techniques for enhancing your effectiveness at interviewing misbehaving children and teens are divided into three sections: creating emotional safety, following the trail of the student's pain, and using high-impact probing techniques.

Create Emotional Safety

When interviewing a student, aim to elicit reciprocity and congruence. You want the student to talk freely to you (reciprocity) rather than merely listening to you. And you want the student to give answers that are relevant and emotionally honest (congruence). The following suggestions will help establish the kind of emotional climate that encourages any student to be more open, trusting, and self-revealing.

Provide A Student-Oriented Setting

To effectively open the door to communicating, provide a student-oriented reception area. Include teddy bears and soft toys for younger children, easy-to-solve puzzles, furniture of appropriate size, and age-appropriate student-oriented reading materials.

Use The S-H-E Greeting

The greeting is very important. Use the S-H-E approach:

S Give a warm **SMILE**.

H Offer a touch or **HANDSHAKE**.

E Make **EYE CONTACT** with student.

Your friendly greeting should include stating your pleasant anticipation of talking with the student and your sincere interest in being of help. If the student is accompanied, look directly at the student, not the other person, as you explain your plan for conducting the interview. For example:

> *"I'm going to talk with your mother first. Then I'd like to talk with you."*

Use A Calm Voice

Your tone of voice should establish your presence not only as a kind and caring individual who is concerned, but also as a firm, valid force to be reckoned with. Never use an apologetic or syrupy tone of voice that would convey insincerity and self-doubt. Never advertise uncertainty by adding "OK?" when you say what you want to do next.

Clearly express your purpose and role. Word the explanation so the student understands that certain adults (teachers, parents) are concerned that he/she might not be as contented or successful as possible:

> *"Your teacher has asked my advice on what she can do to make sure you're as happy as possible at school and that school is pleasant for you. But I can't give her any advice until I talk with you and find out your ideas about what would make school more enjoyable."*

Acknowledge The Student's Discomfort

A student might feel pressured to participate in the interview. He/she might feel attacked, blamed, or treated unfairly by adults. It is crucial to empathize with these feelings and to legitimize any unpleasant feelings the student is experiencing. Don't allow yourself to be perceived as one more oppressor. Ask:

> *"Is your arm being twisted to come and talk with me?"*

If the student responds in the affirmative, empathize with the discomfort:

> *"There have been many times when I had to go places and do things that I didn't want to. I understand how uncomfortable this might seem to you. I'll try to make our conversation as pleasant as possible."*

Disclaim The Three C's

Reassure the student that you're not trying to control, criticize, or change him/her. Your goal is to understand, inform, and help. You want to understand how the student feels and what his/her needs, wants, and opinions are. You want to provide helpful information to the student about what can be different and what better options he/she might choose when deciding how to act. You also want the student to become as contented and successful as possible at home and at school. Most children and teens feel it is safe to talk openly with a friendly adult whose chief desire is to understand, inform, and help. A typical introductory statement would be:

> *"I want you to know that I'm not interested in trying to criticize you, control you, or change you in any way. What I want to do is make sure you're as happy and successful as possible, and I want very much to understand exactly how you feel about things and what your opinions are. I want to understand your viewpoint on some things, because I have some*

information that might be helpful for you. Basically, I just want to help you get the most out of your experience here."

Help The Student Feel Important

By appealing to the student's knowledge and your corresponding lack of information, you inflate his/her sense of personal power during the interview and lower his/her defenses. Acknowledge that you're uninformed and that the student has important knowledge that you greatly respect:

"I can't advise anyone until you tell me what your opinion is. I'm not there, so I don't know what goes on in that classroom for you. But you are *there, and I want to understand exactly what you notice about the other students and about Mrs. Jones. You need to tell me so I can help things work out better for you."*

Make Room For Nonverbal Expression

Children vary greatly in their ability to accurately describe feelings and wants. A simple drawing activity may be especially appropriate for a young under-expressive student. Provide plenty of crayons and a large sheet of art paper. Ask the student to draw a pleasant picture, such as something he/she likes to do, or a picture of his/her family having fun together. The topic of the drawing isn't as important as the fact that the student is preoccupied with the act of artistic creation and is opening up emotionally at the same time. Talk with the student as he/she draws, and avoid overemphasizing your response to the drawing. Keep your focus on the interview and let the student draw.

Follow The Trail Of The Student's Pain

As you track the emotional pain the student is experiencing, envision yourself as a bloodhound on the trail of something important. Unmet needs and emotional pain always underlie misbehavior and often accompany malfunctioning.

Invite Further Comment

Whenever you perceive an indication of emotional pain, follow up with further inquiry:

> *"It sounds as if Mrs. Jones hurt your feelings. Tell me more about what happened yesterday."*

Welcome Tears To The Interview

Tears are welcome third parties during any interview. Invite them into the conversation and give them a voice. Offer tissues and empathy, and reassure the student that your office is always a safe place for tears to visit.

> *"I notice that there are some tears in your eyes when you talk about what happened on the playground yesterday. If your tears could talk, what would they say right now?"*

If the student expresses embarrassment at crying, say:

> *"Nobody's laughing at you now."*

If the student apologizes for crying, say:

> *"This is the safest place in the world for your tears."*

Use High-Impact Probing Techniques

Here are some specific suggestions about how to word your inquiries and comments in order to obtain the maximum amount of helpful information from the student.

Use Student-Level Wording

Use simple and understated expressions and as many one-syllable words as possible. When discussing emotions, stay within the rhyming trio of *sad, mad,* and *glad.* When interviewing a young student, use terminology that appeals to children: magic wands, secrets, wishes, and pretending, for example. Use wording that expresses the student's behavior choices as some form of self-talk. Here are some sample interview questions:

> *"How do you feel deep down inside when Mrs. Jones tells you to stop talking to your friends in class?"*

> *"What do you secretly tell yourself inside your head just before you decide to not do your seatwork in Mrs. Jones's class?"*

> *"When you're in Mrs. Jones's class, are you more mad or more sad? Which feeling is closer to how you secretly feel?"*

> *"If you could pretend that you were somewhere else, where would you pretend to be?"*

Probe For Opposites

Clarify the opposite dimensions of the student's answers. If the student talks of feeling good about something, find out what he/she feels unhappy about:

> *"You said you enjoy playing with your brother most of the time. When* don't *you enjoy playing with him?"*

Probe For Extensions

Suppose you ask:

> *"How happy are you with how life is going right now?"*

And the student answers:

> *"I don't have any big problems. I'm pretty happy."*

Then probe for the extension:

> *"I'm glad you're pretty happy! But you didn't say you're* completely *happy. What would have to change in order for you to be completely happy?"*

Probe For Clarifications

To get a student to elaborate on an answer, probe for clarifications. Use two-option choices where possible: Such probing minimizes distortions in your understanding of the student's feelings. It also teaches the student to use greater clarity when describing feelings, an import life skill to refine.

> *"When you say you don't like Mrs. Jones as your teacher because she never calls on you, I want to be sure that I understand exactly how you feel. Do you mean that she* never *calls on you, or that she* seldom *calls on you?"*

Re-Ask For Validation

Whenever you uncover something you want to explore further, ask the same question in different words. Explain that you just want to be sure you understand correctly. Check the validity of your impression by waiting a few minutes, then re-asking. This method also provides a measure of the student's consistency and lets you confront involved adults with greater confidence about the information you obtained:

> *"Let me make sure I'm understanding you correctly. You said a few minutes ago that you really don't like Mrs. Jones because she hardly ever calls on you in class. And you told me that there are no other reasons why you dislike her. Am I understanding you correctly?"*

Offer Closed-Option Choices

Ask yes–no and multiple choice questions, inviting the student to choose whichever answer is closest to his/her feeling or opinion. Some counselors have been advised not to use this strategy and warned that it limits the range of answers and puts words into the student's mouth. I believe such concerns are usually unwarranted and that the closed-option choice is a good strategy to use. Children and teens generally aren't good at giving elaborate answers to questions about feelings. They appreciate the structure and simplicity of closed-option choices. If the options you offer don't cover enough potentially correct answers, the student will tell you. You may also add "none of the above" as an additional choice. For example, you might ask:

> *"Some students would have felt embarrassed in that situation. Others*

would have felt a little confused but not embarrassed. Which one is closer to how you were feeling?"

"Kids who visit one of their parents every other weekend often feel either very sad, very glad, or very mad about having to visit. Which feeling is closest to how you feel, deep down inside, about visiting your father—sad, glad, or mad?"

Ask Open-Ended Questions

Open-ended questions are effective only to the extent that the student is self-aware and eager to express feelings. There's no need to resort to closed-option questioning if the student is eager to express sincere emotion and frank opinion.

"You said you wanted to talk with me about Sarah. What would you like to tell me?"

Ask Grade-Report Questions

Grade-report questions allow you to probe in many topic areas with a high likelihood of a valid response from the student. You may ask for gradings of just about any person, and even institutions like *this school* or *your family* or *this neighborhood.* When asking the student's evaluation of something or someone, use the grading system with which he/she is familiar:

"Give your mother an A, B, C, D, *or* F *on how well she shows you that she loves you."*

Follow up by probing for clarification:

"You gave her a B. *What does she do that shows you that she loves you enough to earn a grade as high as a* B?"

You may also use the probing-for-opposites technique. A student who assigns a *D* or *F* is experiencing starkly negative feelings. Explore those feelings with further inquiry. Even when the student has awarded a relatively high grade, there is room for probing:

"You gave her a B, *so you decided that she didn't quite deserve an* A. *What would she have to do differently to earn an* A?"

Ask Magic Wand Questions

An interesting and powerful method of assessing areas of conflict and concern is to ask how the student would wish things to be different. This type of question gives you the luxury of probing into specific areas the student might not otherwise think to mention. Request wished-for changes in how people act, what they do, and what they say. Include the student's own self-interest at the end of the question:

"Pretend you had a magic wand and could wave it and change something about your teacher – how she acts, what she does, or what she says. What are two or three changes about her you would make in order for school to be better for you?"

You may need to remind the student that the wand is magic, so that the persons affected would automatically cooperate in making the wished-for changes. If the student claims not to be able to think of any possible improvements, say:

"Just take some guesses. This is a fun question, and the wand is magic."

Magic wand questions provide many useful indications of stresses and issues that are troubling the student. The changes and improvements he/she wishes for are the flip side of the emotional pain he/she is experiencing. After the student states desired changes, follow the pain:

> *"You said you would change your teacher so she would call on you more often during class. How do you feel when she doesn't call on you?"*

Ask "What Are Some" Questions

Instead of asking for *the most...the worst... the best,* ask for *some of the most...worst... best.* Allowing the student to answer with *some* gives him/her much more psychological room to respond than asking for a specific, polarized answer.

> *"What are some ways in which you think your teacher could improve things for you at school?"*

is a much better question than:

> *"What is the most important way your teacher could improve things for you at school?"*

This second version forces the student to run an election for *the most* prior to giving you an answer and is, therefore, an ineffective probe.

You can easily come up with several good *What are some...* probes:

> *"What are some...*
>
> > *things you like to do with your (mother/father/sister/grandparent/teacher)?"*
> >
> > *ways in which your (mother/father/sister/grandparent/teacher) is better to you than (some other person)?"*
> >
> > *ways in which your (mother/father/sister/grandparent/teacher) is not nice to you?"*
> >
> > *things you would try to get out of doing with your (mother/father/sister/grandparent/teacher) if you could?"*
> >
> > *things you like best about your (mother/father/sister/grandparent/teacher)?"*

Inquire About All Major Relationships

Ask magic wand questions about the student's interactions with parents:

> *"If you could wave a magic wand and change some things about your mother—how she acts, what she does, what she says—what would you change about her to make your life better?"*

Repeat the same question about the full range of significant others in the student's life, including parents, step-parents, siblings, and teachers. Aim for obtaining at least three changes, then ask follow-the-pain questions to clarify student needs exposed by the magic wand questions. Ask magic wand questions of the student's significant others and compare their answers with those given by the student. Ask the student's perception of such factors as the C and D percent (page 33), misbehavior cycles, and the frequency of piggy-backed messages from parents and teachers.

Use grade-report questions to establish an understanding of how the student perceives he/she is treated by significant, involved adults. Your questions can usually revolve around how the adults show love to and discipline the student:

> *"Give your teacher an* A, B, C, D, *or* F *for how well she shows you that she cares about you."*
>
> *"Give her a grade for how fair she is to you when you bother the student next to you."*

Ask About Unfairness

Simply asking for ways in which adults are treating the student unfairly is another useful technique.

> *"In your opinion, what are some ways in which your teacher is unfair to you?"*

Ask About Wishes

A particularly powerful way to focus in on psychological pain the student is experiencing is to ask a vague question that invites a thoughtful answer about what he/she wishes there were more and less of in his/her life:

> *"What do you wish there were more of in your life? What do you wish there were less of in your life?"*

CHAPTER 4

Understanding & Counseling The Misbehaving Student

Assess Family Relationships

Children and teens must relate to three spheres involving peers: school, social relationships, and siblings.

You can obtain useful information from involved adults about the student's adjustment in all three spheres of peer relationships. In addition, it is usually beneficial to interview siblings as well as the student.

Siblings may have been pushed out of the limelight because of continued misbehavior or other problems involving the student. If so, they especially appreciate your interest in their opinions and observations. Remind them that they are in an excellent position to observe interaction between the student and their parents and that you greatly value their opinions. Most siblings are very receptive to such an affirmation of their importance.

Interviewing siblings simultaneously with the student allows you to observe their typical interactions. It also gives you the benefit of an instant double-check on the accuracy of what the student tells you during the interview. If you interview siblings while the student is in the room, ask them to comment on and clarify information you receive from the student. Talk directly with the student, checking from time to time with siblings about what the student has just told you. Do they agree? Can they add information for you?

If significant sibling rivalry exists, questions about parental fairness to the student as well as to his/her siblings will uncover it. Suppose Mark is the problematic student. Ask his siblings:

> *"In what ways do you think your parents are unfair to you because of how they treat Mark?"*

Ask the siblings grade-report questions about how well their parents show love to the student as well as to them. Ask additional grade-report questions about the fairness of parental discipline. Ask whether the siblings think their parents are making any mistakes in how they deal with the misbehaving student. Ask what advice the siblings would give their parents about changing how they deal with the misbehaving student. You may also conduct very specific probes:

> *"In what ways do you think your (mother/father/step-parent) favors Mark over you?"*

> *"In what ways do you think your (mother/father/step-parent) treats Mark differently from how you are treated?"*

To assess strengths and weakness in sibling relationships, consider adding such inquiries as:

"What are some...

things you especially like to do with your (brother/sister)?"

things you dislike having to do with your (brother/sister)?"

ways in which your (brother/sister) bugs you the most?"

things you admire and respect about your (brother/sister)?"

things that bother you about how your (brother/sister) acts?"

The Privilege-Resentment Cycle

The privilege-resentment cycle spurs misbehavior and involves the student's day-to-day interaction with siblings. Ask the siblings about its existence and about how each family member intentionally or unintentionally contributes to it.

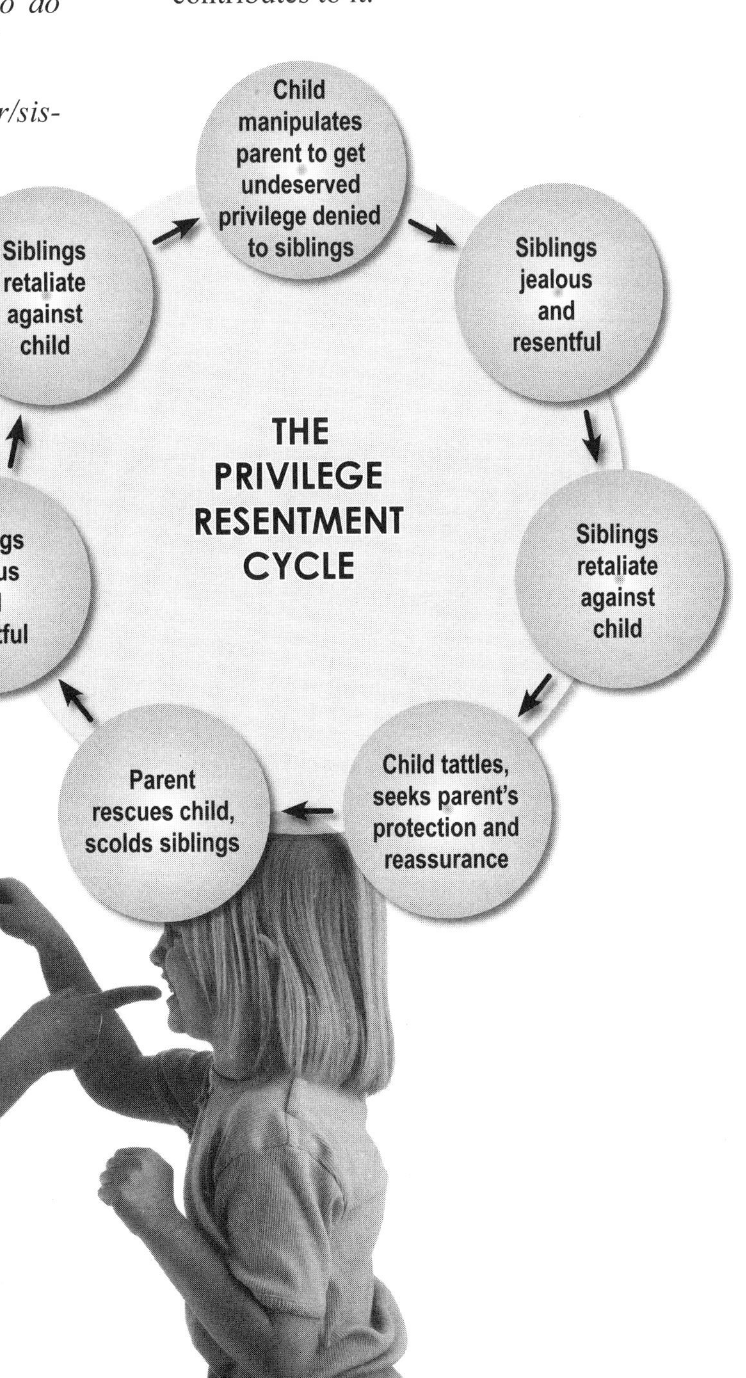

Family Stress Map

This powerful technique provides an overall view of family conflicts in a brief period of time. Use it with several or all family members present.

Draw The Family Map

Represent each family member with initials or his/her first name inside a small circle on a whiteboard, chalkboard, drawing easel, or similar apparatus. Include non-custodial parents if they have regular contact with at least one child in the family. Arrange these circles within a larger circle.

Connect The Circles

Connect the circles with lines. Explaining that each circle represents a family member, say:

> *"Each person in your family is connected to everybody else and has a relationship with everybody else. The lines represent the relationships within your family."*

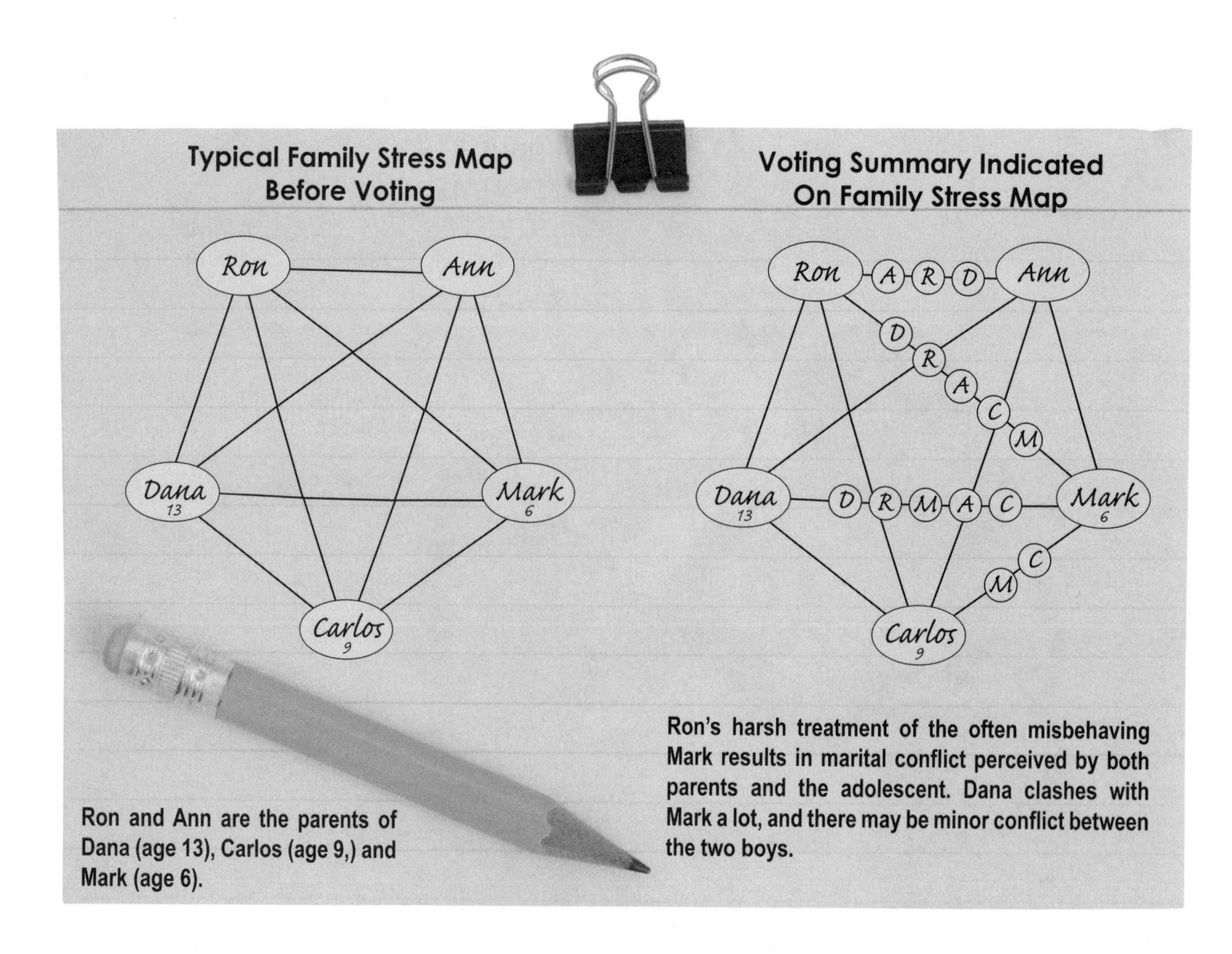

Ron and Ann are the parents of Dana (age 13), Carlos (age 9,) and Mark (age 6).

Ron's harsh treatment of the often misbehaving Mark results in marital conflict perceived by both parents and the adolescent. Dana clashes with Mark a lot, and there may be minor conflict between the two boys.

Conduct Conflict Voting

Starting with the oldest child, say:

> *"Of all the two-person relationships indicated by the lines, please vote for the three that, in your opinion, involve the most conflict, stress, and hassle."*

It is usually helpful to reiterate that a voter may choose any lines, including lines to which he/she is not connected. Mark the three lines with the initials of the person selecting them. Proceed in identical fashion with the other children and, lastly, the parents. Leave preceding votes on the board as you elicit new votes. Limit your request to three votes, regardless of how many circles comprise the family diagram.

While I have found that children under the age of 6 are usually unable to respond to this form of inquiry, exceptional younger children may be able to give reliable answers. Remind young children to vote their own opinions, not just vote as their siblings voted.

Isolate Key Conflict Relationships

After everyone has voted, summarize the results. The three or four relationships most often selected become the focus of your further interrogation. You now have two important sets of information: the configuration of family stress patterns and the key conflict-laden relationships.

Use Stress Pattern Data

Point out that many high-conflict lines connect the circles of certain family members. One of these family members is likely to be the student you're assessing. Take advantage of this opportunity to enhance your rapport with him/her:

> *"Look at how many lines are going to you! I think you're under more stress than anyone else in your family!"*

Such empathy is the virtual opposite of the kind of feedback the student has been receiving. He/she expects to be criticized and labeled a *troublemaker.* However, your introductory comments to the student included your statement that you were not interested in criticizing. Your quick display of empathy can go a long way toward facilitating a cooperative relationship with the student and family.

If the line between the parents was selected as one of the key conflicts, the couple's relationship may be contributing to the student's problems.

Gather Information From Stress Avoiders

Family members whose lines were not selected are *stress avoiders.* These individuals are excellent sources of observation about the other, more-stressed relationships. Ask how they manage to avoid getting involved in high-conflict issues.

You might discover that a stress-avoider is the *angel* in an *angel-brat* sibling relationship with the misbehaving student. When sibling rivalry and competition within the family are extreme, children tend to polarize their roles and conduct themselves in vivid contrast to each other. Motivated by rivalry with the misbehaving student and perceiving opportunities to exploit the student's antics, *angel* siblings can appear very obedient, cooperative, and innocent. At the same time, they try to make sure they are given credit for their angelic behavior and are eager to point out how much *better* they are than the misbehaving student. More-determined angels may even goad, urge, dare, or trick the misbehaving student into acts of further misbehavior, then quickly tattle. An angel's ultimate goal is to gain special status with his/her parents. These manipulations, however, can be as destructive to peace and harmony as the misbehavior of the student you are assessing. The angel's halo shines so brightly, it's hard to see the horns inside it.

Gather Scenarios Of The Key Conflicts

Examine each of the key stressed relationships by asking the family to describe typical scenarios. Who usually starts the conflict? How does each of the two persons contribute to it? For example:

> *"You voted for the relationship between your mother and Amy. Please tell me about a typical conflict between them. Who usually starts it and how? What happens next? How does each person make it worse? How does it finally stop?"*

Use the family stress map to obtain the student's opinions about conflict patterns within the family. Use all the types of questions explained in this section to elicit information about sibling issues.

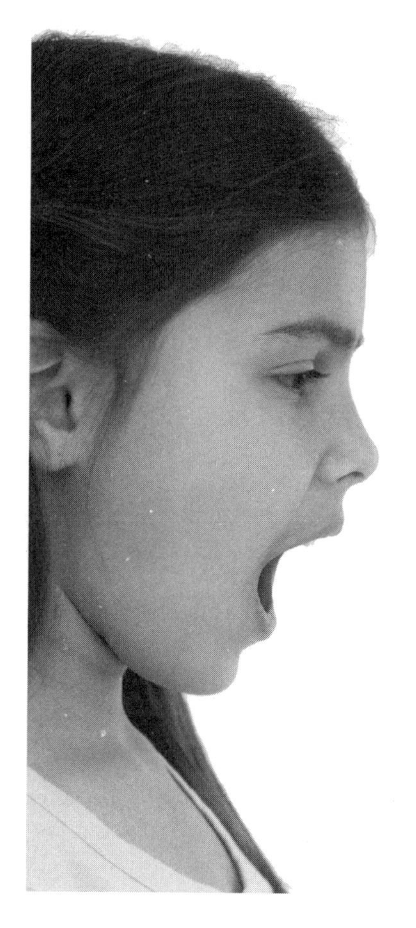

Examine each of the key stressed relationships by asking the family to describe typical scenarios.

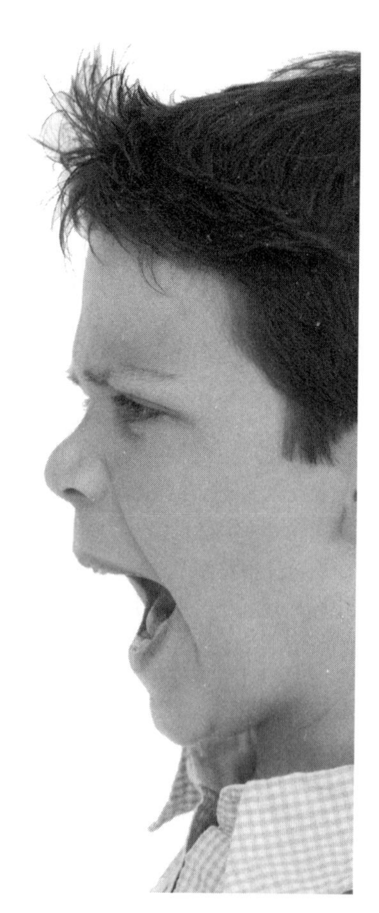

CHAPTER 5

Understanding & Counseling
The Misbehaving Student

Assess Self-Concept

Self-concept, like misbehavior, tends to be self-perpetuating and to obey one of Newton's *Laws of Motion.* Unless acted upon by significant outside influences, these traits proceed in the direction in which they are moving.

The student who self-applies the label *uncreative,* for example, hunts for evidence to support that assumption and dismisses potentially encouraging messages to the contrary from well-intentioned teachers and parents. Two students reminded that an important assignment is due the next day will interpret the teacher's reminder in two different ways. The encouraged, optimistic student will conclude, "My teacher likes me and wants me to do well!" The discouraged, pessimistic student will conclude, "My teacher's picking on me again!"

Self-Concept Questioning Techniques

The Top-Of-The-Mountain Question

One effective way to obtain an idea of a student's overall perspective about life is the top-of-the-mountain question:

> *"If you were standing on the top of a mountain and had a special microphone so you could talk directly to (the whole world/all children/teens everywhere/all parents everywhere/all teachers everywhere) what would you say about how you really feel about (life/school/living in your family)?"*

Open-Ended Questions

Some additional useful open-ended inquiries for assessing self-concept include:

> *"What are some of...*
>
> > *your favorite TV shows? What makes them so enjoyable for you?"*
> >
> > *your favorite heroes? What makes them special?"*
> >
> > *your favorite books? What makes them special?"*
> >
> > *your earliest memories?"*
> >
> > *your hopes for the next (month/year/semester)?"*
> >
> > *your favorite things to do?"*
> >
> > *the most important things you think about?"*
> >
> > *the things you think about most?"*
> >
> > *the things that bug you most about (school/family/life, etc.)?"*
> >
> > *the biggest difficulties, hurdles, and challenges facing you right now?"*
> >
> > *the things you worry about most?"*
> >
> > *the thoughts that scare you most?"*

The Magic Wand Question

The self-applied magic wand question is also a useful technique:

> *"If you had a magic wand and could wave it and change something about yourself (how you act, what you do, what you say) what would you change about yourself to make life better?"*

The Lie Detector Question

It is helpful to probe for clarification and opposites after receiving answers to the magic wand question and the open-ended questions. Use this follow-the-pain question:

> *"If you were hooked up to a lie detector and had to tell the truth, what would you say are your chief weaknesses or things about you that aren't as good as they could be?"*

Lifestyle Motto

An interesting way to assess any student's self-concept is to ask for his/her life-guiding beliefs, often referred to as a *lifestyle motto*. This technique is suitable for those who have at least reached preadolescence, but is too difficult for younger children. Interview parents to obtain their opinion as to a young child's life-guiding beliefs. Ask preadolescents and teens directly.

Introduce the activity by saying:

> *"I'll write a brief phrase, then I want you to write on your paper some words and phrases that reflect what you believe deep down inside about that topic."*

After writing each phrase on the board, allow about a minute for the student to respond. Ask the student, or parents of a young child, to supply words and phrases that correctly describe his/her life-guiding motto. The phrases are:

After writing "The world is…" ask:

> *"In your opinion, what kind of world do you live in? What words or phrases describe it?"*

After at least a minute, write "People are…" and ask:

> *"What words or phrases describe the kind of people who populate this world outside your circle of close friends? What are they like?"*

After writing "I am…" ask:

> *"What words and phrases describe your chief traits and characteristics? What makes you unique and different from other people. What traits are important aspects of being you?"*

After writing, "To survive, I must always…" ask:

> *"Given the way the world is, people as they are, and you as you are, what must you do to survive in this life?"*

A lifestyle motto of a well-adjusted student would be something like:

> *The world is an exciting and interesting place.*
>
> *People are kind, trustworthy, dependable, nice, helpful, and caring.*
>
> *I am capable, competent, valuable, unique, and loved.*
>
> *To survive, I must always treat people kindly so they'll be nice to me.*

A lifestyle motto of a less well-adjusted student would be something like:

> *The world is scary, unpredictable, overwhelming, boring. It sucks.*
>
> *People are untrustworthy, hurtful, mean, selfish, deceitful.*
>
> *I am hurt, weak, victimized, angry, scared, bad, a show-off.*
>
> *To survive, I must always* (description of acting-out).

The fourth sentence, "To survive I must always…" is usually a description of acting-out and often reflects one or more of the five goals of misbehavior. Answers to the fourth sentence fall within the five goals listed on the chart on page 56. Asking directly for the student's lifestyle motto can be a helpful supplement to various other methods of deducing the goals of misbehavior.

THE FIVE GOALS OF MISBEHAVIOR

Goal 1:
STRIVING FOR NURTURE AND AFFIRMATION

To survive, I must always...
- get all I can
- show everybody how smart I am
- make everyone notice me
- get them to accept me
- act like a clown in class
- show off
- make them like me

Goal 2:
KEEPING PEOPLE AT A DISTANCE BY CONTROLLING AND DOMINATING

To survive, I must always...
- make sure they never get the best of me
- lie to keep them confused
- make sure I'm always right
- never let them boss me or tell me what to do
- get into arguments
- show them who's boss

Goal 3:
HURTING OTHERS TO DRIVE THEM AWAY SO THEY WON'T ATTACK

To survive, I must always...
- hurt them before they hurt me
- be ready to fight
- make them afraid of me
- be the toughest guy around
- beat 'em up

Goal 4:
AVOIDING RESPONSIBILITY AND WITHDRAWING FROM CONTACT

To survive, I must always...
- tell them to go away
- stay stoned
- get all the drugs and beer I can
- not try any more
- smoke pot
- give up

Goal 5:
CREATING EXCITEMENT DESTRUCTIVELY

To survive, I must always...
- find something exciting to do
- stir up some excitement
- pull stunts to keep them off guard
- get into mischief

CHAPTER 6

Understanding & Counseling The Misbehaving Student

Why Misbehavior Involves Goals

Continual misbehavior indicates imbalance in important aspects of the student's life. Uncovering areas in which the student is lacking, needful, or unfulfilled provides meaningful clues to the mechanisms underlying the misbehavior.

If the areas of unfulfillment are interpersonal, four common patterns occur. These goals or purposes of misbehavior can target peers, adults, or both. All four patterns involve manipulating and exploiting people and forcing an intended social result. Any specific instance of misbehavior can involve more than one of these goals, though one usually predominates. Some chronically misbehaving students consistently pursue two or thee of the five goals. The fifth goal is intrapersonal in nature.

Stemming from a break in any of the five links in the *Chain of Encouragement*, these five common goals or purposes of misbehavior can be referred to as:

Goal 1: Connection-Seeking

Goal 2: Power-Seeking

Goal 3: Revenge-Seeking and Hostility Display

Goal 4: Avoidance of Responsibility and Participation

Goal 5: Destructive Excitation

Recognize Unmet Needs

For insight into what the student is trying to accomplish, notice the circumstances and immediate domino effects of the misbehavior. The emotional (inward) and behavioral (outward) manifestations by the student and by affected others are crucial sources of information. They indicate areas in which the student feels unfulfilled and, therefore, the purpose or goal of the misbehavior.

The student's mood, energy level, facial expression, and body language while misbehaving and immediately afterward indicate much about underlying needfulness.

The misbehavior or malfunctioning the student displays is a compass needle that points directly at the underlying unmet need. Ask yourself "What is this student trying to get other people (teacher, classmates, counselor, parent) to do or feel?" The answer will be a tip-off to the student's needfulness.

The first step in helping lift a student out of misbehavior is to determine which goal he/she is pursuing.

Feelings Experienced

The student's mood, energy level, facial expression, and body language while misbehaving and immediately afterward indicate much about underlying needfulness. While misbehaving, the student may exhibit any of a broad range of emotions including such states as anger, sadness, confusion, desperation, dependence, or embarrassment.

Message Conveyed

Misbehavior says something to the world in general and to involved adults and peers in particular. The same type of action conveys different messages in different settings. Each unique message must be analyzed in terms of the misbehavior's specific context. But each message almost invariably reflects the student's discouragement with him/herself or with life. Most misbehavior is a misguided attempt to experience greater personal power in the face of these perceptions. There is usually a driven, compulsive quality to the message the student is conveying.

Initial Support Or Enabling From Adults

There are generally two types of first-impulse responses by adults:

1. falling in line with or accommodating the student's intentions
2. blocking or opposing the student's intentions

Regardless of type, first-impulse responses tend to perpetuate the problems. Do the involved adults seem to *oppose* by showing anger, repelling the student, overwhelming the student with their own power display, showing a desire to get revenge on the student, acting bewildered, seeming discouraged, or becoming despondent about the student? Such enabling responses sustain or magnify the student's misbehavior, regardless of the adult's stated intention

Student's Response To Adult Enabling

A further confirmation of the misbehaving student's intended purpose comes from his/her response to adults' enabling messages. If the same misbehavior continues, its purposes will be even easier to identify.

Initial Confrontation By Adults

When adults' initial responses oppose the student's intention, an *ignore-nag-yell-punish* sequence can develop. While not directly sustaining the misbehavior as enabling responses do, these relatively inefficient actions trigger their own set of problems and counter-responses from the student. The readily recognizable patterns that emerge contribute to an understanding of the student's purpose in misbehaving.

Hunt for the domino effects on involved adults. What are their feelings and emotional responses to the student? Adult responses often reflect the nature of the discouraged student's actions and will help point to the student's underlying needfulness. Be especially watchful for involved adults' excessive, polarized, cyclic, or extreme emotional responses to the student.

Spurred on by feelings that occurred in response to the misbehaving student, involved adults tend to choose actions that further indicate the student's underlying unmet needs. These first impulses, which might be regarded as involved adults' emotional knee-jerk reactions, are usually accurate guides to what the student is trying to get adults to do. Later responses from adults are likely to be more reasoned and more therapeutic.

As with emotional components, involved adults' actions in response to the misbehaving student may vary considerably from one situation to the next. In any individual case, there may be considerable exception to these general trends. Watch for cycles and repeated occurrences that settle into a predictable pattern involving sustained conflict.

Student Response To Adult Confrontation

When an involved adult responds to the misbehaving student with a firm but ineffective first-impulse confrontation, the ensuing exchange escalates difficulties. The results provide additional clues to the purposes of the misbehavior. Gather scenarios for these types of interactions, because they are helpful intervention guides.

Student Response To Adult Goal-Labeling

When the adult correctly labels the goal of the misbehavior, the student suddenly intensifies eye contact or breaks off any existing eye contact. Accompanied by a shift in arms, legs, or overall body position, this *recognition reflex* is easily identifiable during a student interview. This phenomenon confirms the adult's identification of the student's purpose in misbehaving.

Goal 1: Seeking Connection Through Social Interaction

If the first link in the *Chain of Encouragement* is broken, the student who does not experience sufficient contact, interaction, affirmation, acceptance, or attention will misbehave in ways that force contact with or service from others. The student has a secret belief that the only way to "count" is to obtain undue contact, attention, interaction, or service.

Students who don't feel enough of the first link attempt to attain their desire by misbehaving in various ways. How about the student who shows off with wisecracks, smart-aleck remarks, silly antics, or bragging? Not having enough of the first link, he/she wants to coerce and trick people into interacting more with him/her. How about the pest who forces the teacher to stop teaching in order to nag or scold? The student who acts helpless and tricks the teacher into giving excessive service is also fishing for more contact. A more pathological version would be the student who lies about a terrible event that allegedly occurred and garners huge amounts of attention and concern from well-meaning but duped teachers, counselors, and classmates.

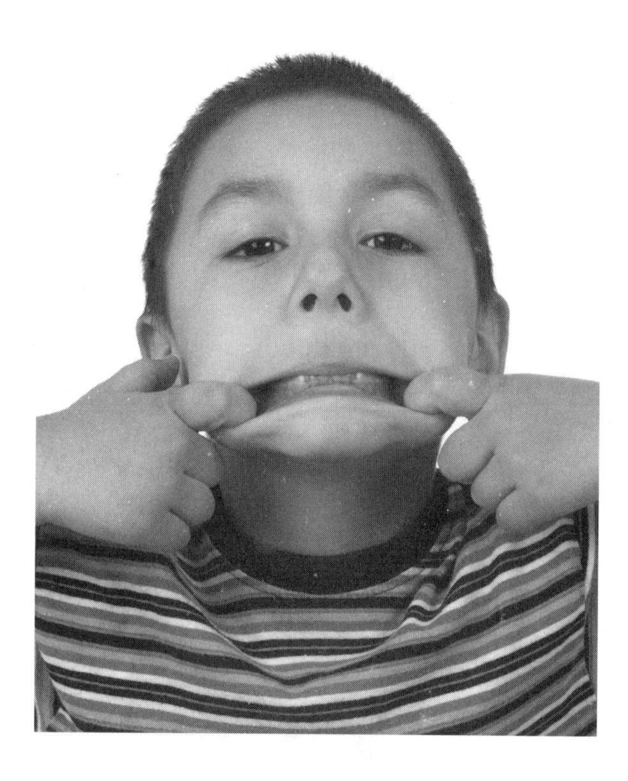

Response From Teachers

In response to the showing off and clown-like antics of the attention- and interaction-seeking student who needs more of the first link, expect teachers' initial responses to involve:

- nagging the student about numerous aspects of classroom behavior
- waiting on and paying excessive attention to the student
- shooing away a bothersome, intrusive student
- frequently telling the student to stop misbehaving
- frequently referring the student on disciplinary matters
- scolding and criticizing the student's antics
- accusing the student of arrogance and showing off
- feeling tricked into paying attention to the student
- feeling disgusted by the student's apparent arrogance and need to show off
- feeling annoyed and bothered by the student's antics
- feeling drained from re-teaching and re-explaining to the student

Goal 2: Seeking Power

The second link in the *Chain of Encouragement* sometimes breaks, causing the student to experience insufficient ability to influence day-to-day activities. Or he/she may feel unable to protect him/herself from being dominated or coerced into behaving a certain way. To compensate for these types of stressors, the student misbehaves in ways that force a power showdown.

The student's secret belief is that the only way to "count" is to display personal power.

The student's secret belief is that the only way to "count" is to display personal power. Students who don't feel enough of the second link want to display their power. Those who insult and put down classmates are taking arrogance to another level. It is an attempt to feel powerful, and a reflection of a need for more of the second link. How about the debater who acts like a future lawyer in the presence of adults or the blatantly defiant student who tricks adults into endless arguments and power struggles? Or the student who tells adults one thing, then acts-out his/her own wishes behind the adults' backs? This sneaky, passive-aggressive student is making a power play, too. The tendency to be bossy while at play is another reflection of needfulness based on inadequately experienced personal power (the second link). The dominating student who orders playmates around and elects to play with those who are younger is also searching for excessive and illegitimate power.

Response From Teachers

When a student who needs more of the second link exhibits bossiness and invitations to power struggles, expect teachers' initial responses to include:

- trying to force or coerce the student into behavior changes
- speaking to the student in a raised voice
- punishing the student
- arguing with the student
- feeling challenged to display more authority
- getting tricked into power struggles
- feeling exhausted by frequent debates and endless arguments
- making threats in order to control the student

Goal 3: Seeking Safety Through Hostility And Revenge

Sometimes the third link in the Chain of Encouragement breaks and the student feels a need to obtain much more of a sense of being safe, loved, and respected. Being rejected, abused, neglected, or otherwise severely victimized often causes a student to misbehave in ways that hurt others. Misbehaving for this purpose is testimony to the pain and oppression the student feels as well as to his/her inability to comfortably witness others' success and apparent happiness. The student is an emotional *have-not* who can't stand to witness the contentment of the *haves*. The best defense is a good offense. The student's secret belief is that the only way to be safe is to drive everyone else away.

Students who don't feel nurtured and protected and don't experience enough of the third link sometimes attempt to extract evidence that they are loved from the adults in their lives. In this way, they may seem very much like students who are hunting for more attention and service. Students whose basic need for safety is unmet as a result of having been abused, bullied, or violated are likely to put almost all their coping energy into a desperate attempt to be safe from further attack. They adopt a revengeful posture toward their parents, then toward the world.

The original target for the student's revenge is almost invariably one or more parents. Caught up in this attempt at emotional survival, adults at school become victims the student tries to bully. In general, the more offended the faculty and staff become, the more intensely the student attempts to cause disruption. A powerful way to hurt teachers is to disrupt their attempts to teach and to distract other students from participating. At school, the student displays a hostile attitude with profound disrespect to authority figures of any kind. He/she makes insulting remarks and describes teachers, topics, and classmates in derogatory and profane terms.

There is, however, a proactive aspect to the hostility. The student tries to look tough, act tough, and be tough so he/she won't be hurt any more. Not only does the student care little about academic performance at school, he/she also becomes the playground bully. These bullies comprise a large proportion of juvenile delinquents. They are likely to pick on such weak targets as younger children. At high risk for not developing a conscience, they are likely to show little or no empathy for their victims and can become violent at school.

The hostile student usually has two major issues. One has to do with being academically uncooperative, under-productive, and non-participatory. It is often a spin-off of the more pervasive, more serious second issue: a revenge posture toward the world. Caring little about how anyone else feels, the student wants to rain on everyone's parade and spit in everybody's soup.

The revenge-oriented student doesn't have any constructive energy to devote to worthy enterprises like academic effort. Even the act of being civil or courteous may be beyond this student's comfort zone. Being asked to study hard, devote time to a homework assignment, or participate in class discussion may seem like giant intrusions into the student's very fragile sense of selfhood and a drain on his/her personal energy supply. These requests represent a subtraction from the student's available coping energy But too much has already been taken from him/her in an abusive manner.

The student's disruptive antics reflect an attempt to feel safe from being violated, victimized, or hated. The tragically misguided game plan is to alienate and frighten everyone in sight so that nobody will want to try to hurt him/her any more. Looking and acting tough ends up as a lose–lose situation in many ways. Unable to trust, the student surrenders any willingness to enter into emotional partnerships.

In alienating everyone else, he/she is attempting to become a psychological hermit. He/she must then attempt the impossible task of making sure all his/her needs are met with no assistance from anyone. Severing this connection ruins the student's ability to develop much of a conscience. As the student proceeds down the path of delinquency, this course leads to disaster of awesome dimensions. It ends in incarceration. In a misguided attempt to hurt his/her parents, the student succeeds in hurting him/herself, family members, and peers in many ways.

Response From Teachers

Teachers' initial response to hostile and vindictive actions of the student who needs more of the third link generally include:

- feeling rejected by the student
- feeling threatened and in danger of being the victim of student violence
- feeling hated and regarded with disdain by the student.
- being protective of other students victimized by the revengeful student.
- punishing the student
- scolding and criticizing the student
- taking offense at the student's words or actions
- sobbing because of being hurt and insulted by the student

Goal 4: Seeking Comfort Through Avoidance

A student with a broken fourth link in the Chain of Encouragement sometimes experiences disheartening frustrations at school- or home-based tasks, activities, and obligations. This is especially true of those involving a challenge. When done successfully, such activities would raise self-esteem and provide a sense of personal competence and importance. In response to these perceived insufficiencies, the student misbehaves in ways that force others to stop making performance-based demands. The student has a secret belief that the only way to "count" is to appear successful by avoiding the disclosure of any personal weakness.

This behavior results in a collection of traits that indicate a tendency to avoid responsibilities. Here are tip-offs to hunt for.

Refusing To try

The student might refuse to try earnestly or risk imperfect performance. The misbehavior reflects an attempt to be relieved of feeling incompetent. He/she chooses to avoid responsibility and to avoid participation in stressful activities. It is less painful for a discouraged student to get a low grade because he/she didn't try at all than to get a low grade after making his/her best effort. Perhaps you know some students who play hooky, have numerous unexcused absences, don't do seatwork or homework, or in other ways shut down and stop trying. Hunting for any excuse to avoid facing the difficulties inherent in effort, they might even flaunt their incompetence and use it as an excuse.

Challenging Adult Standards

Another way to avoid feeling the sting of incompetence is to challenge adults' rights to demand performance in the first place. Students who reject adult standards and societal norms are often attempting to withdraw from pressures to perform. They might identify with rock stars or rap stars, professional wrestlers, motorcycle gang members, or street gang members whom they perceive as defying parents' or teachers' standards of decency and appropriate behavior.

Claiming Special Exemption

Students who don't experience enough of the fourth link feel unable to handle the tasks presented to them. Sometimes they go a step further and begin to believe that they are incompetent, stupid, or entitled to special exemption from the responsibility of trying or participating.

Seeking Frivolous Preoccupations

Students who are deep into an avoidance pattern tend to engage in one shallow and frivolous activity after another. They often are highly discouraged and lack sufficient self-confidence to face the academic challenges at school. Avoiding responsibility and participation means focusing instead on pleasure and frivolous activity. The apparent lack of effort is not so much a search for fun as a desperate, self-protective avoidance of challenge.

Giving Up Quickly

For the student who has been exposed to extraordinary stresses or overwhelmingly negative life experiences, there is a great risk of becoming an avoidant student. Assertion blocked for a long time results in anxiety or tension. The child carries on an internal debate of great ambivalence on the order of "Assert! No, don't assert!" Children stop asserting for their needs when it becomes either unsafe or unprofitable to continue. A form of despondence sets in. The net result is a pervasive *I give up* attitude.

Exclusively Social Motivation

Secretly embarrassed by his/her low level of coping energy, the avoidant student faces an awful choice:

- make an honest effort at school and suffer through getting mediocre or low grades that reflect the poor quality of work he/she has energy to produce

- insulate him/herself from that pain by adopting an *I don't care* attitude.

Most avoidant students choose the second option and attend class in body only, not in mind or spirit. This student is likely to be simultaneously operating under three guiding mottoes: "I can't do it," "I don't care," and "I give up." All three propel the student away from having any effective relationship with the teacher. Intimidated by the prospect that he/she might make embarrassing mistakes, the student becomes a perfectionist, inhibited about making an honest try at challenging tasks of any kind. The pervasive nature of the student's lack of resilience to stress and work pressure is often hard for parents, educators, and helping professionals to grasp. An act as seemingly mundane as attending class or doing a few math problems can seem utterly overwhelming to the student. School is reduced to a social experience, with almost the totality of the student's interests being directed toward schoolmates rather than toward academic participation.

Leave Me Alone Attitude

Equal to the attraction to low-productivity peers is repulsion from authority figures. The avoidant student wants teachers to go away and leave him/her alone. When confronted about this attitude, the avoidant student gives rebuttals such as:

- Don't worry about it.
- It's my problem.
- I'll take care of myself.
- So what?
- It really doesn't matter.
- It's my business.
- I don't care.
- I give up.
- Leave me alone.
- I don't want to talk about it.

Using Time Unwisely

While insistent on claiming personal space and freedom, the avoidant student almost never uses them constructively. Instead, he/she makes a project out of avoiding all constructive efforts. Life becomes a whistle-stop tour of triviality, perhaps flitting from one meaningless and shallow entertainment to the next in a constant effort to avoid being truly responsible or dutiful. This student attempts to fill vacant hours with equally vacant activities.

Profound Pleasure-Seeking

Seldom, however, is the avoidant student aware that fear of facing responsibility is at the core of under-productivity at school. All he/she is likely to be aware of, it seems, is liking to spend time doing whatever he/she feels like doing. This self-serving pleasure-seeking is part of a more encompassing trait. So pervasive is the quest for pleasure that the student is likely to become extremely narcissistic and hedonistic, often to a self-destructive degree.

Depression is more likely to occur in the avoidant student than in any of the other four types of under-productive students.

Being Pessimistic

Sometimes the avoidant student becomes angry at him/herself and eventually may have trouble accepting any positive messages. He/she may discount them or explain them away as accidental or coincidental successes. Wallowing in self-rejection, the student can become bitterly pessimistic and unhappy about life. Perfectionism again provides negative input, and the student is constantly dissatisfied with whatever little attempts he/she makes at school. Depression is sometimes the next step.

Depression

Depression is more likely to occur in the avoidant student than in any of the other four types of under-productive students. Watch for these tell-tale indications. If you notice any, immediately refer the student to a skilled mental health professional or agency.

Many of these signs can occur because of reasons other than depression, and some are the direct effects of various psychiatric medications. School personnel should identify these problems and refer students for further scrutiny by a mental health professional.

The following are indicators of depression in children and teens:

- irritability
- loss of emotional control
- decreased interest or pleasure in most activities
- failure to obtain pleasure from would-be pleasurable activities
- apathy or an indifferent attitude about many things
- decreased appetite, loss of interest in eating (not due to medication), skipping meals
- greatly disturbed sleep pattern (not due to medication)
- fatigue
- insufficient energy for normal activities
- expressed feelings of personal worthlessness
- talk of running away
- marked indecisiveness
- marked deterioration in ability to concentrate and think through issues
- frequent sobbing or crying
- suicidal thoughts or plans

Even more serious than depression is the possibility of an imminent suicide attempt. The avoidant student, more than any of the other four types of uncooperative students, is at risk for committing suicide.

Be on the alert for any of these indications of a serious suicidal gesture. They don't always occur, but they occur often enough that they can serve as telltale indicators of suicidal intent. If you notice even one of them, take action immediately. The student who is determined to kill him/herself in the near future will often give one or more of these four tip-offs, easily remembered by the acronym RAGS:

R: Reveals elaborate plans

Many teens make vague suicidal threats, but some carry their intentions to a fatal level of preparation. One of approximately every 100 vague mentionings of a suicidal thought results in death. What differentiates this special mentioning is that it unveils a scheming, plotting, planned execution of the act of suicide. The student reveals to a friend, for example, that he/she knows where he/she will obtain the pills he/she will use, what he/she will include in his/her suicide note, who will discover his/her body and when, who will find the note and when, and other similar intricacies.

A: Anticipates D-day

The student acts as if everything will be fine after a certain date in the near future. The suicidal teen suddenly appears calm and happy for no apparent reason. He/she has determined his/her Death Day.

G: Gives things away

The student gives away or sells such valuable personal property as clothing, CDs, videos, a DVD player, or a television set. He/she might also try to give away mementos and sentimental items.

S: Says *good-bye*

The student contacts friends and loved ones through e-mail, notes, phone, texting, or personal conversations. Be especially alert for a list of names and phone numbers.

Response From Teachers

Teachers' initial responses to misbehavior that reflects irresponsibility and participation avoidance may include:

- feeling baffled by the student's negligence
- frustration at the student's unwillingness to try
- feeling confused by the student's resistance to assistance
- despair because coaxing fails to bring about improvement
- pitying the student's obvious self-doubts
- frustration that the student doesn't seem to respond to praise
- persistent urging of the student to try harder
- nagging the student about completing assigned work
- labeling the student as *lazy* and *irresponsible*
- ignoring the student and giving up on attempts to reach him/her
- frequently reassuring the student about his/her ability, intelligence, or competence

Goal 5: Seeking Arousal Through Destructive Excitement

Sometimes the area of unfulfillment is centered primarily on inside-the-self issues having to do with boredom, curiosity, the need to explore and test personal boundaries, or self-definition. The misbehavior usually targets objects that the child or teen abuses, destroys, or takes apart.

This misbehavior is most often due to insufficient stimulation, entertainment, or excitement, or occurs when the student's brain is underdeveloped or under-responsive. The student destroys or improperly uses objects or people in an attempt to satisfy gnawing needs for excitement.

Students who don't experience enough of the fifth link feel bored. When they misbehave, their actions create excitement of a negative, destructive nature. They doodle excessively instead of taking notes during class. Sometimes their misbehavior involves destruction of property and disruptive manipulation of objects. They throw paper wads and carve their initials into desk tops. They mark walls with graffiti. They commit minor acts of vandalism. In more severe cases, they become playground bullies, phone in bomb threats, and create mischief that seriously disrupts classmates' functioning.

Response From Teachers

Teachers' initial response to the disruptive stirring up of excitement by the student who needs more stimulation generally includes:

- feeling bewildered by the student's bizarre, destructive antics
- feeling obligated to keep reminding the student to pay attention
- becoming annoyed by the student's pesky misbehavior and disruptiveness
- frustration at the student's ability but refusal to focus
- nagging the student about numerous aspects of classroom behavior
- frequently telling the student to stop misbehaving
- frequently referring the student on disciplinary matters
- scolding and criticizing the student for misbehavior
- accusing the student of *being lazy* and *wasting time*

CHAPTER 7

Understanding & Counseling
The Misbehaving Student

How To Redeem Misbehavior & Malfunctioning

Students need encouragement just about as often as they need to breathe. A misbehaving or malfunctioning, uncooperative student is discouraged and has chosen one of the two destructive options:

1. He/she can misbehave to get the need met
2. He/she can do nothing to get the need met

To motivate uncooperative students, address their underlying needfulness.

The first step is to aim your intervention toward the correct links in the *Chain of Encouragement* (see page 18). Only after determining which aspects of encouragement are lacking can you accurately choose the corrective techniques most able to encourage the student. Your interventions must be in concert with the specific aspect of discouragement the student is experiencing. Redemptive approaches for the student who is seeking attention (the first link), for example, are quite different from those to assist the revenge-oriented student (the third link). Likewise for the other three links, your approach must harmonize with and directly address the specific needfulness the student is experiencing.

Your goal is to help the discouraged student reject the options of misbehavior and malfunctioning and to introduce a win–win option of appropriate assertion to meet underlying needs. Simultaneously, encourage teachers and parents to discontinue enabling responses and other forms of simply falling in line with the uncooperative student's manipulations.

Reject The Two Destructive Options

Introducing this concept is usually a safe and powerfully effective counseling maneuver:

> Anyone who has a need has three options. (1) He/she can misbehave to get the need met, (2) can do nothing to get the need met and continue to suffer, or (3) can ask for help to get the need met.

Combine this general introduction with a specific example directly applicable to the student. It is hard for any student to disagree when this concept is introduced as part of a counseling session. Once the student understands and accepts the validity of the three-options concept, the way is open to get him/her to agree to work on rejecting the first two. Point out that the first two create lose–lose situations. They both involve painful consequences that don't resolve anything and don't change anything for the better. Elaborate as needed. If possible, draw a specific example from the student's life.

Reject The *Malfunction* Option

The *malfunction* option is relatively easy to dismiss. Start by empathizing with the student's need, then suggest that the malfunction option is simply not acceptable:

To the interaction-seeking student, say something like:

> *"I understand your desire to be noticed, appreciated, and liked. Everyone has such a need. And I agree with you that doing nothing about it is foolish. Suffering in silence doesn't bring about a solution. So I agree with you that sitting in class and simply being sad and feeling lonely and overlooked is not a good idea."*

To the power-displaying student, say something like:

> *"I understand your desire to not be bossed around and to get to have your way sometimes. Everyone has such a need. And I agree with you that doing nothing about it is foolish. Suffering in silence doesn't bring about a solution. So I agree with you that sitting in class and simply being bossed around and powerless is not a good idea."*

To the hostile student, say something like:

> *"I understand your desire to not be a victim of people who are mean to you. Everyone has such a need. And I agree with you that doing nothing about it is foolish. Suffering in silence doesn't bring about a solution. So I agree with you that sitting in class and simply feeling hurt and mad at everyone is not a good idea."*

To the avoidant student, say something like:

> *"I understand your desire to not feel overwhelmed by the assignments your teacher is asking you to do. Everyone has such a need. And I agree with you that doing nothing about it is foolish. Suffering in silence doesn't bring about a solution. So I agree with you that sitting in class and simply feeling as if you can't really do the work is not a good idea."*

To the stimulation-seeking student, say something like:

> *"I understand your desire to be stimulated and to have excitement wherever you are. Many people have such a need. And I agree with you that doing nothing about it is foolish. Suffering in silence doesn't bring about a solution. So I agree with you that sitting in class and simply being bored is not a good idea."*

Reject The *Misbehavior* Option

Once you have dismissed the malfunction option, attack the *misbehavior* option. This step may be more challenging, because understanding any and all acts of misbehavior as lose–lose events will probably be a new concept for the student. Clarify that misbehavior almost invariably starts out as an attractive option. It is disguised as a win–lose event. The student expects to win at someone else's expense. The bully expects to hurt his victim, the clown expects to disrupt the class, and the power-seeking little lawyer expects to trap the adult into a lengthy argument.

To many uncooperative students, misbehavior is very attractive and seems totally appropriate and wise. To a child who is abused, acting tough and mean may seem like the only sensible way to get others to stop attacking. To the overwhelmed child, giving up and not trying may seem like the only wise thing to do in the face of intimidating and difficult academic tasks. You may have an uphill struggle when you try to convey the self-defeating nature of misbehavior to a chronically misbehaving child or teen.

But there is always a *lose* component underneath the apparent *win*. Find it. Talk about it. Do whatever it takes to make the student recognize it. Make sure the student understands the concept of the hidden *lose–lose* underneath the apparent *win–lose* of misbehavior.

The student expects the negative results—the *lose* part of what the misbehaving student expects to be a *win-lose* event—to affect only the target of his/her misbehavior. However, these events affect the perpetrator as well. There is no true win–lose after all—only lose–lose in disguise. The negative effects on the misbehaving student often emerge later, long after he/she gets away with something. Help the student understand this concept.

To many uncooperative students, misbehavior is very attractive and seems totally appropriate and wise.

Use the example of someone shoplifting. The crime is not detected, and the shoplifter enjoys the use of the pilfered item. Where is the *lose* component to the event? It is, of course, in the long-term results, the arrogant belief that he/she can steal successfully in more circumstances. But what is likely to eventually happen to someone who shoplifts again and again? The obvious answer of *getting caught and being incarcerated* is only part of the answer you want the student to verbalize to you. Other aspects have to do with diminished reputation, lessened understanding of how and why to earn a respectable and honest living, and so forth.

Advocate The *Assertion* Option

Therapeutic movement flows easily after dismissing the other two options. Merely introduce the idea that the third option is the only one that makes sense. Point out that it leads to win–win results, resolves the situation, and paves the way for future improvements. Don't get sidetracked into debating whether the misbehavior is *lose–lose* or *win–lose*. Point out that a win–win would eliminate all doubt.

Then ask the gold-mine question:

> *"What could you possibly do in this same situation, starting tomorrow, that would be different and would create a* win–win *solution?"*

Notice the emphasis on the future. Referring to *tomorrow* or to *next time* is always encouraging. The student can't possibly have failed in the future, so it is always safe and uplifting to talk about. The future is also the only time the student has in which to make the necessary improvements in his/her behavior.

How To Counsel The Interaction-Seeking Student

Here are four steps for successfully redirecting the energies of the interaction-seeking student. Using a specific example from the student's known behavior:

1. discuss the various disruptive antics the student is trying to use in order to obtain evidence of being liked, noticed, accepted, or valued

2. focus on the ways in which each specific misbehavior appears at first to be *win–lose* but is actually a *lose–lose* event in disguise

3. brainstorm with the student and list the aspects that are leading to a true lose–lose

4. suggest possible win–win alternatives to replace the student's current lose–lose acting-out

For example, long-term results of disrupting the teacher with wisecracks and gross humor include being regarded as offbeat and, eventually, rejected by classmates. This is the interaction-seeking student's worst fear and the result he/she is trying so hard to avoid. Then suggest possible win–win options from among these possibilities or additional ones unique to this student's circumstances.

Encourage The Performing Arts

Schedule the student in a drama class or work toward involvement in community children's theater. Activities involving theatrical productions are excellent for building a feeling of teamwork among the cast and crew. The performing arts in general are suitable arenas for strengthening any student's feelings of partnership with others. Help the student gain membership in groups, take lessons, or in some other way participate in singing, performing magic, dance, a marching unit, or playing a musical instrument.

Heighten Social Participation

Involve the student in a social-awareness program, small group discussion series, self-concept unit, or similar experience. Teachers can sometimes arrange these kinds of experiences within the classroom setting. Faith-based youth groups, Scouts, Campfire, the local Y, or other youth-oriented and character-building organizations can also be fruitful avenues for helping any student increase friendships and popularity.

Upgrade Social Skills

Work directly with the student by training him/her to acquire needed social skills. These specific behaviors, on the basis of interpersonal contact, tend to gain positive responses from others. After careful scrutiny of the difficulties the student is experiencing in conducting social relationships with peers and faculty, proceed with social skills training. There are three basic types of social skills training: *Mentoring, Counseling*, and *The SCORED Method.*

Mentoring

This method involves learning from an older student who has refined social skills and would be a suitable model. Arrange for the mentor to give feedback to the student and suggestions for improving attempts to elicit attention and interaction from others.

Counseling

This method involves group or individual discussion and practice of the needed social skills. A group setting offers several advantages, including the opportunity to role-play the skills and obtain instant feedback as to their effectiveness.

The SCORED Method

Interspersed with actual application in the classroom and at home, this six-step instructional method assists the student over a brief period of time. This method may be used in a group as well in an individual format, Each session should last less than 15 minutes.

S: Show

Demonstrate the skill by acting it out for the student. Make sure the student pays attention to your body language as well as to your words.

C: Coach:

Describe the skill step by step. Instruct the student in how and when to use it. Explain how it provides short-term and long-term benefits, and how it leads to a win–win outcome. Show why the skill is important and point out the negative results that occur when it isn't performed properly. Convey enthusiasm about the skill, and optimism that mastering this skill will help the student feel a greater sense of belonging and connection with others.

O: Offer self-reminders:

Provide self-talk statements to guide the student in how and when to use the skill. These self-talk messages are silent personal prompts to be used whenever the student attempts to use the skill. The student will cling to them in stressful moments, so make them simple, catchy, rhyming, or otherwise easy to remember. Overstate and simplify rather than being too technical. For example: "Raise my hand? Yes I can!" or "When I want attention, ask for it by raising my hand" and "Zip my lip."

R: Rehearse:

Have the student role-play the skill in a simulated, realistic situation. You may, of course, also role-play privately with the student or during a group-counseling session or a friendship club meeting in your office. Give the student feedback about how he/she is doing. Practice until the student develops credible poise and performs with smoothness and an easy flow.

Be open to the use of prepared scripts, reminder cards, mirrors, audio- or videotaping, or using any other device that will help the student. For some students, it might be better to contrast the right way to perform a social skill with role-plays of various incorrect applications of it. You might want to include role-plays of potential surprises that might occur, unusual or offbeat occurrences, and other variations until the student develops instinctive, accurate judgment about what to do. The instant feedback provided in a group setting is quite useful for this step.

E: Encourage:

You have introduced and demonstrated the skills and provided self-talk reminders and rehearsals. Now you're ready to send the student forth to apply the skill in genuine social settings within home, neighborhood, or school environments. In most cases, the new setting is a classroom. Make an appointment to talk with the student about the results of his/her attempts. When you meet, give the student permission to be imperfect:

> *"When we met last Thursday, you were going to raise your hand in Mrs. Smith's class during the next seven days rather than call out. I noticed you were in her class today. Tell me the good news and the bad news about what happened. First tell me some good news."*

Notice the deliberate endorsement for bad news and the stated preference to hear the good news first. This encourages openness and honesty from the student and indicates your healthy emphasis on progress, rather than perfection. It also prevents *best foot forward* lying in order to impress you.

D: Debrief:

Invite the student to continue to expand and refine his/her social skills. The goal is to have him/her experience subtle victories that build self-confidence, so arrange frequent debriefing meetings. Schedule several of these meetings during the first week, but keep them brief. Each meeting should last no more than a few minutes. Comment favorably on the student's attempts and correct any aspects needing refinement. Give plenty of encouragement, express confidence in the student, emphasize the progress he/she has made, and share his/her joy about getting attention in new and better ways.

Strengthen Friendship Skills

Blatant attention-seeking misbehavior at school sometimes reflects a basic need to feel more popular and better accepted by peers. If you suspect such a motive, try working directly on upgrading the student's ability to make and keep friends. Find out how many friends he/she has, and what activities he/she shares with them. Ask what the student's friends would say they don't like or they wish were different about the student. Let this information guide your interventions.

Combine counseling, discussion, and instruction to teach the following friendship skills. Make sure the student is applying each of them correctly in social settings, at home, and in classroom and playground interactions with peers. Have the student copy this list of friendship secrets and place it where he/she can see it daily. Also have the student make a copy on a small card to carry throughout the day for quick review at any time. Modify the wording as needed to adapt to the student's age and level of language mastery.

Find More Friends

The student needs to consider expanding his/her friendship network.

> *"Instead of standing alone on the playground, join in when your classmates play games. Help them see that you want to be their friend. To meet potential new friends, get involved in the Y, parks, clubs, Scouts, Campfire, church youth groups, music lessons, sports teams, exercise or dance classes, art lessons, bowling leagues, gymnastics martial arts classes, or similar groups."*

One At A Time

If the student's home is not a safe place for potential new friends to visit, perhaps you can create a friendship club that meets at the school counselor's office.

> *"The best way to make new friends is one at a time. Invite a potential new friend into your home to share some fun activity."*

Talk About Their Topics

To attract and hold the legitimate interest of peers in normal interactions, the student must learn to become more other-centered in conversation.

> *"Rather than remaining silent, talk with your potential friend. Make him/her feel good by talking about topics that interest him/her. If you talk only about yourself, the other person might think you're boring or too interested in yourself."*

Get Them To Talk About Themselves

Few topics attract others' interest more effectively than getting them to talk about themselves.

> *"Show your potential friend that you're interested in learning about him/her. Ask questions so he/she wants to answer you. Find out what he/she likes to do and other interesting things about him/her. Show interest by looking into the other person's eyes when he/she talks with you."*

Care About Their Feelings

Showing empathy is always a powerful way to enhance others' willingness to interact.

> *"If your friend has good news, show that you understand how happy he/she is. If your friend is unhappy, show that you care."*

Use The Politeness Words

The student must learn that politeness enhances social attractiveness.

> *"Polite words such as please and thank you are great tools for building friendships. Use them a lot."*

Smile

Research has verified the common-sense observation that children who smile often are inherently more socially attractive.

> *"One of the best ways to attract friends is to show your happiness to them. Your smile is the most beautiful thing you can wear."*

Guests First

The student must demonstrate other-centeredness in terms of allowing peers to take the first turn.

> *"Your potential friend will like you more and be happier if you let him/her go first when you play."*

Guests Get To Choose

Some children are unpopular because of being too bossy. The student must show other-centeredness in terms of allowing peers to exercise their options. Peers don't want to be bossed.

> *"Your potential friend won't want you to boss him/her. Let your friend choose what to play, what snack to eat, or what DVD to watch."*

Use The *Half-And-Half* Rule

Another way to decrease bossiness is to introduce the idea that each child controls only one-half of the event.

> *"You each make half of the choices. If you and your potential friend are playing with toy dishes, say: 'You place your dishes on this side of the table and I'll place my dishes on that side.' You may also use this rule to help decide what to play: 'First, let's play what you want. Then we can play what I want'."*

Use The *Right-To-Stop* Rule

Willingness to break off an activity when the other person starts to tire of it is an important social-awareness skill.

> *"You each may stop the game at any time. When one of you is tired of playing the game, both of you start on another activity. Neither of you tries to control the other."*

Teacher Interventions For The Interaction-Seeking Student

The student who needs more of the first link is probably gaining undue and excessive attention and interaction from the teacher and from classmates. These corrective responses have worked well for some teachers:

- Assign more partner work.
- Involve the student in small-group discussions.
- Involve the student in whole-class activities to which every student contributes, such as creating a mural or making a quilt.
- Personally greet and welcome the student each day. This is an unbelievably powerful way to improve a discouraged student's attitude and warmth toward any teacher.
- Publicly acknowledge his/her services.
- Address weak friendship skills.
- Arrange to have lunch individually with each student in the class some time during the school year.
- Place the student in a prominent position so others get to know him/her and so he/she performs pleasant services for which others feel grateful.
- Have the student distribute papers to classmates, run an important errand, and make announcements over the school loudspeaker.
- Suggest specific win–win ways to obtain attention in the classroom. Teach the needed social skills.

By combining these interventions, you can help lead the interaction-seeking child away from misbehavior and uncooperativeness and toward a much healthier position within the social milieu.

How To Counsel The Power-Seeking Student

The power-seeking student presents a great challenge to school personnel when he/she shows noncompliance toward teachers and administrators. This student's primary goal is to experience strength by successfully opposing authority figures at school.

In general, the best way to counsel a power-seeking student is to make it clear that you won't get involved in power struggles.

In general, the best way to counsel a power-seeking student is to make it clear that you won't get involved in power struggles. State right away that you're not interested in criticizing, controlling, or changing the student. Clarify that you are interested in understanding, informing, and helping:

> *"I want you to know right from the beginning that I'm not interested in doing any of the Three* C's *with you. I'm not going to criticize you. I'm not interested in trying to control you, and I don't want to force you to change.*
>
> *"Instead, I want to do three other things. First of all, I want to understand exactly how you feel, how you see things, what your opinions are on a number of issues, what your wants are, and what you think would be best. The second thing I want to do is share information that I think might be interesting or helpful to you. My third goal is to help you get along better ...enjoy school more ... stop getting into trouble in class ...*

By disclaiming contentiousness and proclaiming your intention to understand and help, you stand a better chance of having the student be frank with you and listen to you. Converse with the student until you obtain a clear idea of the nature of the autonomy he/she wants to have at school. It will often involve wanting more control over time, the nature of assignments, or the teaching style used by the faculty. Then help the student find more appropriate ways to attain increased autonomy.

Arrange For Built-In Autonomy

Increase the student's sense of personal power to make and influence choices within the classroom. Most methods used to accomplish this step require the teacher's active participation and are discussed later. The debate team might be a feasible arena for the teen who wants to experience personal power by proving how right he/she is. Perhaps the physical education teacher can structure noncompetitive play experiences as part of an enlightened curriculum. Participation can teach the power-seeking student and his/her classmates the joys of cooperation as an alternative to coercion and competition.

Teach Negotiation Skills

Show this student how to negotiate. He/she needs to learn how to obtain *cooperation* without resorting to *coercion.* He/she can also teach such skills to peers by becoming a peer counselor. Perhaps there is a teen court in your community.

Encourage *Despite* Logic

The power-seeking student's stubbornness can sometimes be used to advantage. It is generally a good idea to support any student's agency (choice-making power). Invite the student to use this kind of self-talk:

> *"I'm going to get my education, despite the way the teacher is. Just because the teacher acts that way doesn't mean I'm not allowed to enjoy my schooling or get an education. I refuse to let that teacher rob me of the benefits of an education."*

As another example:

> *"I won't let Mr. Foltz's unfairness control whether I enjoy my schooling or participate in my studies. I refuse to give him that much power over me."*

Take Advantage Of Natural Consequences

If the student remains uncooperative despite your attempts at accommodating his/her need for power, let natural consequences unfold. Results such as low grades remain the student's problem, but you are always willing to talk about ways to make school more enjoyable. Reaffirm your intention not to engage in senseless power struggles or arguments:

> *"I won't argue with you about whether you're going to do your work. That's something only you can decide. I'm not going to try to control you or make you do anything. You have to decide when the consequences of your actions are so obnoxious that it's time to change how you approach things here at school. Nobody can make that judgment for you.*
>
> *"I'm not going to try to make you change. I want you to know that I'm rooting for you. I'm not here to criticize you. I hope you'll decide to make the most of you learning opportunities here at this school. I'll be available to talk with you any time about how to improve how things are going."*

Give The Lose–Lose Insight

Discuss in detail the various disruptive antics the student uses to try to feel more powerful as an individual. Discover the lose–lose behind the apparent win–lose of each tactic. If the student bosses classmates and insists on being first, there will be insufficient practice at such essential socialization skills as showing humility and taking turns. The long-term results of this behavior include resentment and rejection by classmates. The student will be unprepared for and unhappy with instances when he/she can't be first or be the boss. Trapping teachers and parents into arguments and power struggles may create a temporary feeling of power, but provides little preparation for the necessary life skills of *negotiation* and *peaceful relating to others*.

Sidestep Power Struggles

Avoid enabling the student's manipulations through mistakenly entering into power struggles. Here are some methods to help you sidestep an invitation to engage in a power struggle. Use this approach directly with the student, and show parents and teachers how to use it.

- Isolate the conversation.

  "I have something special to discuss with you. Can we meet for a minute after class?"

- Remain non-judgmental. If you haven't caught the student at the misbehavior, don't accuse him/her on circumstantial evidence.

  "I wasn't there, so I don't know whether you've done this. But I have a concern."

- Acknowledge influence without total control. Remember that one of the first things to say to a power-seeking student is that you aren't trying to control or change him/her.

  "I can't control you and I don't want to."

  "I'm not handcuffed to you."

  "I have too much respect for you to try to MAKE you do it"

- Start with the student's wants and needs.

  "What can we do so that you'll want to do things differently next time?"

  "If you could determine how everything goes, what would you like to see different about this situation?"

- State your feelings clearly, completely, and honestly.

  "If you do it the way you say you want to, I would feel..."

  "Doing it entirely your way would create a problem for me."

- Set limits and conditions to your cooperation.

  "Here's what I propose. I'll make you a deal. I won't assist any student who speaks to me in an unkind tone. When you're ready to discuss this seriously, I'll be here."

- Get permission to state your desire about the student's actions.

  "May I share with you what I wish you would do about this?"

  "Would you like to hear what I think is best for you to do?"

- Indicate your refusal to engage in a power struggle.

  "I'm not going to argue with you about this. I want a peaceable solution."

  "I won't engage in a power struggle with you about this. I'm simply not going to try to settle this with an argument."

- State exactly what you wish the student would do differently.

  "What I think would be best for everyone is that you..."

  "How about if I do this and you do that?

  "What I wish you would choose to do is..."

- Insist on a win–win solution.

  "The only solution I will accept is a win–win."

  "You're too valuable to be part of anything but a true win–win solution to this problem."

  "You deserve a win–win solution."

- Keep the door open for further discussion.

  "I want you to know that I'm always willing to renegotiate."

  "Let's talk about this again after we've tried this win–win solution."

  "I'm always happy to talk with you to make any solution more of a win–win."

  "Let's explore this issue more later."

These methods can significantly lessen the chaos a power-seeking student imposes upon a classroom. Adhere to the *Three C's* promise and find open channels through which the power-seeking student can legitimately experience increased power and decision-making opportunities. Refuse to enter into power struggles, and encourage the student to transform stubbornness into a determination not to be dissuaded from benefiting from school.

Teacher Interventions For The Power-Seeking Student

The student who needs more of the second link is making lose–lose attempts to exercise greater personal autonomy. The teacher can use better methods than such first-impulse responses as direct power showdowns and arguments. The teacher should follow your example of sidestepping the student's invitations to engage in a power struggle. The key is to channel the student's bullheaded determination in constructive directions. Teachers can help transform power seeking into leadership and positive contributions to classroom atmosphere and processes by:

- finding ways to increase the student's perception of his/her personal influence and increase his/her decision-making scope
- teaching a unit on *arbitration* and *negotiation skills*
- inviting the student to do extra-credit reading and give a report or presentation to the class on the topic
- establishing a classroom atmosphere conducive to student participation and shared decision-making
- having regular class council meetings
- giving students a range of options for earning grades and passing the course
- putting the student into high-status and leadership positions

- inviting the student to become more involved in student government
- arranging for the student to lead a class discussion or chair a committee
- inviting the student to conduct a survey or write an article for the school newspaper
- having the student run an important errand
- complimenting the student on his/her intensity, determination, leadership ability, and willingness to stand up for what he/she believes
- inviting the student to become involved with volunteerism or with a school-community liaison program

How To Counsel The Hostile Student

The roots of this type of misbehavior are intertwined with family issues. Your loftiest goal is to help this student get beyond the bitterness to tolerance or forgiveness, a feat that even adults do not often accomplish. Successful intervention with a deeply hostile student may require such intense, sophisticated approaches as individual and/or group psychotherapy for the student as well as for family members. In terms of less-intense interventions, start with establishing rapport and work on developing a relationship of trust.

Free From Pathological Relationships

Show the student that his/her would-be friends are willing to double-cross him/her or otherwise behave in hurtful ways. If the student's parents appear to be part of the problem, find legitimate activities to keep the student away from his/her parents and in the company of inspiring, helpful adults during after-school hours.

Provide A Healthy Relationship

Find a suitable surrogate parent figure with whom the student can experience a nonabusive, trusting, emotionally safe relationship. Perhaps there is a coach, favorite teacher, Scout leader, church youth group leader, someone from the local Y, or another suitable person in a position to adopt such a role. Simply having regular contact is enough. So a music teacher, dance instructor, martial arts instructor, recreation director at the local children's gym, or other adult role model will do.

Give The Lose–Lose Insight

Help the student declare emotional independence from his/her oppressors, who may include a parent. Begin by giving the student insight into the mechanism behind his/her hostile attitude. Determine whether this student feels hurt, violated, or shortchanged by life and is purposely under-performing at school for revenge. If so, show your empathy and concern. Use the student's self-centeredness in the service of self-change by introducing the notion of his/her making a crucial mistake:

> *"I understand why you feel violated about some of the things life has handed you. I would be very angry at anyone who treated me the way you've been treated. But I think you're making a crucial mistake.*
>
> *"Your mistake is aiming your anger in the wrong direction. You want your teachers to be upset so they'll feel bad. You think you're pulling off a win–lose. But what you're doing is sabotaging your own education. The real victim seems to be you more than anyone else. Being victimized is the very thing you're trying to escape."*

Refute The Game Plan

Show the student how his/her tragically misguided game plan to alienate and frighten everyone in sight hurts him/herself in many ways. He/she would be better off trying to make true friends who won't hurt him/her and who will help see that his/her needs are met.

Encourage Martial Arts

Martial arts instruction, if well taught and focusing on self-control, is sometimes helpful with this type of student. Once the student has confidence in his/her ability to defend him/herself, there is no longer a need to display toughness like a badge. Many martial arts programs require adults to sign cards indicating that the student is displaying the codes and tenets (character traits) of the program before the student can advance to the next level or belt.

Refute The Faith In Revenge

Directly refute the student's belief in revenge. Point out that two people in an ongoing revenge struggle both suffer and nothing is actually decided. Revenge is self-perpetuating, with each person continuing the struggle immediately after receiving the last blow from the other person. Clearly, a revenge struggle is a lose–lose enterprise.

Uproot Perfectionism

Underneath it all, the vengeful student is a perfectionist. He/she is making a ridiculous and impossible demand that everyone treat him/her perfectly fairly in every circumstance. Confront this perfectionism. If the student is ever to break out of this mentality, he/she must acknowledge that nobody is perfect at anything.

For a persuasive visual aid, use the half-filled-glass demonstration. Fill a transparent glass approximately halfway with any liquid. Ask the student to describe the liquid level. Get him/her to say that the glass is half full or half empty. Point out that the top half is *emptiness* and the bottom half is *fullness.* Then draw the analogy to life:

> *"This glass symbolizes what happens to each of us every day. Every time anybody talks to us or does anything to or with us, it is a mix of fullness and emptiness. Or, you might say, good news and bad news."*

Find a concert featuring the student's favorite musical group or another event the student would enjoy participating in or attending. Discuss the positive and negative experiences that would occur while preparing for, traveling to and from, and attending the concert. Then introduce the notion that there are two ways to handle the inevitable emptiness of life:

> *"People have two basic options. They can have a tantrum every time anything isn't perfect: 'How dare this situation or that person be imperfect toward me!' Or they can say, 'That's the way life is. I'll focus on remembering and enjoying the positives, and just let the negatives go. I know they're always going to be there anyway, so why get upset about them?'"*

Apply this logic to the concert analogy. The student would enjoy the concert more by taking a camera, having pictures for a scrapbook, and remembering the songs he/she heard and the fun he/she had. He/she would have happier memories if he/she forgot about the traffic, the expense, the long walk from where he/she had to park to his/her seat, the long wait before the concert started, and other inconveniences or annoyances. Most people prioritize memories this way. Invite the vengeful student to try it.

In addition to this useful notion of accepting imperfection rather than demanding perfection, introduce the concept that *positives* are more important than *negatives.* Most people have learned to revere and cherish the positives while dismissing or not getting upset by the negatives. Use the dying-in-the-desert analogy:

> *"Suppose you've been lost in the desert for three days. You are dying of thirst. Seeing a tree that will provide shade from the burning sun, you stagger to it and plop down, exhausted. Much to your amazement, a sign in the sand under the tree says "For emergency use" and has an arrow pointing downward. You notice that the sand at the base of the sign appears moist.*
>
> *"You dig into the sand and discover a canteen. You shake it and realize it has liquid in it. You hope it is drinkable water. You unscrew the cap and find pure, fresh water, about halfway*

up. Do you say 'Aw, it's half empty!' and throw it away?"

Coax as needed to get the student to acknowledge that the *fullness* part is more important than the *emptiness* part. Then use real-life examples to help him/her apply that truth to life in general and to his/her life in particular. This half-filled glass demonstration can sometimes provide a counseling breakthrough by providing a hostile student with a sensible framework for being more tolerant and forgiving.

Teach Insulating Self-Talk

To deal with teasing and harassment, treat each incident as an opportunity to teach important facts to both participants. A teaser who wants nothing to do with the child or teen should not make teasing comments. If the teaser is actually fishing for more contact, suggest better ways of making contact than by harassment.

Here are useful self-talks to help the student deal with being teased in ways other than by trying to get revenge:

Magician's Trick

When a magician does a trick, everyone except me is amazed and excited. If I know how the magician does the trick, I'm not excited about it at all. In the same way, I know how the teaser does his trick—he/she is trying to make me feel sad by using words. So I'm not going to let him/her trick me. I'm going to be unexcited and unimpressed by his/her trick!

Powerless Words

There is no power in the words the bully uses. Words can never hurt me. They only come into my ears through the air, and they don't hurt my ears. Words can hurt me only if I decide to let them hurt me. So I'll decide NOT to be hurt by them!

I'm In Control

The teaser wants to force me to be sad. But I won't let the teaser control how I feel or whether I'll be happy or sad. *I'm* in charge of me and I will decide how happy or sad I'm going to be.

Do The Opposite

The teaser wants me to feel sad. So I'll do the opposite and feel happy. That way, I'll be sure not to do what the teaser wants!

Who Has The Problem?

I know how to be happy, and I'll stay that way. I know that the best way to be happy is to help other children become happy. The teaser thinks that the way to be happy is to try to make other children (like me) sad. The teaser is wrong! So the teaser will never be happy. The words the teaser aims at me are only a tiny problem. But the teaser has the big problem of not knowing how to be happy.

The Secret Wish

The teaser's secret wish is to talk with me and play with me. That's why the teaser is trying to upset me. I can show the teaser a better way to make friends and get others to play. The better way is to share things and offer to play. Maybe the teaser will say *yes,* and both of us can have a fun time!

Tell Them To Stop

Announcing clearly and honestly the need for the other person to stop irritating actions is an important part of learning how to confront others. A three-part message provides a universal method of defining personal needs for others: The child or teen states how he/she feels, asks for what he/she needs in order to feel better, and makes a win–win deal with the other person. The entire statement would be something like:

> *"When you do that, I feel frustrated and confused."*
>
> *"Please don't do that; do this instead."*
>
> *"If you do it that way, I'll do what you want in a few minutes."*

If the child or teen has trouble with the entire three-part message, substitute such a basic assertion as:

> *"That bothers me; please stop it."*
>
> *"Please don't do that to me."*
>
> *"Please stop doing that."*

For a younger student, introduce the statement as a special *trick* or *magic phrase* to use whenever the child senses a build-up of frustration about what others are doing.

Teacher Interventions For The Hostile Student

Hostile students and avoidant students share several similarities. They are often more emotionally at risk and hamstrung by pervasive psychological and emotional issues than the other three types of misbehaving students. Of the five types, hostile and avoidant students have the least coping energy to devote to constructive efforts at school. So they are unlikely to show much diligence or efficiency at performing seatwork, turning in homework, or studying for tests. Whereas interaction- and power-seeking students crave high-energy transactions with the teacher, hostile and avoidant students try to remain emotionally disconnected and deflect teacher interaction. Wanting to be left alone, they may become openly hostile if the teacher attempts to put too much pressure on them to perform or interact.

In addition to avoiding power struggles with the power-seeking student, the teacher must avoid being drawn into revenge cycles with the hostile student. Students who are uncooperative at school because of a deeply violated sense of self usually have little coping energy available for academic effort or even for courtesy toward the teacher. The major battle must be fought, deep within the child's psyche, by a partnership between the child and a skilled mental health professional. The teacher is usually more of a potential victim than a significant agent for therapeutic improvement.

Your major, and perhaps only, admonition to the teacher is that he/she make two sincere efforts to:

- protect classmates from the revenge-oriented student's vindictiveness
- mute his/her own responses to any attempt by the student to offend him/her

You are basically advocating that the teacher become a scientific observer of, but not a participant in, the student's manipulations. Give this explanation to the teacher:

> *"Imagine this student performing a magic trick to impress an audience. You are backstage and can see how he/she does the trick. You are not impressed, and you aren't emotionally moved by the trick. In the same way, consider his/her crude statements and offensive antics as attempts at performing a trick on you. Don't be in the audience. Be backstage. Notice what the student is doing, and choose to be unimpressed and unmoved."*

How To Counsel The Avoidant Student

Like the other four types of misbehaving students, the avoidant child or teen has concluded that congruent assertion of needs is not a viable option. Intervention with this type of misbehavior should center around bolstering coping ability and providing encouragement.

Give The Lose–Lose Insight

Discuss with the student how his/her disruptive antics reflect attempts to relieve pressure to perform for an authority figure. Show how at school these behaviors lead to lose–lose results affecting not only the student, but his/her classmates as well as the teacher. At home, they lead to lose–lose events with family members. By not participating, the student is depriving the other students of whatever insights or clever ideas he/she might have been able to contribute. By trying to avoid anything dutiful and inconvenient, the student is failing to prepare for life. Life is never free of duty or inconvenience. All the while, the student is learning very little at school and is literally wasting his/her academic, social, and personal life.

Use the following demonstration in counseling the student. It illustrates that all growth and improvement involves risk and effort. Ask the student to stand near you with his/her eyes closed, then say:

> *"Pretend that you have to go through life like that. What is the one way to make sure you will never stub your toes or your heels?"*

Coax as needed to get the student to say that he/she should never move. Then say:

> *"You'll be very safe, but also very stuck!"*

Explain how *being safe* and *being stuck* are practically synonymous. Help the student understand that trying to remain stress-free by not trying also means being stuck in terms of not learning, not advancing, and not developing needed skills. We can't ask that life not require risk. This concept adds clout to your portrayal of the fact that this student is currently choosing a lose–lose option.

Watch For Depression

One of the most challenging quandaries mental health professionals and school counselors face is dealing with a depressed and potentially suicidal student. You will want to take action immediately, but which actions? With whom should you communicate? What about confidentiality issues as well the right of the student's parents to be informed? What if you hear about potential suicidal intention from a reliable source close to the student, but the student denies it? These concerns must be thought through ahead of time; response procedures may differ from one school district to the next. Local, state, or provincial regulations may also vary in terms of procedures required during potential or suspected suicidal ideation.

It's generally wise to include at least these five easily remembered steps, which spell the acronym *A FACT*:

A ADDRESS the future

The suicidal student is saying, "I have no future." Your response should be to make a case for there being a future. Use anything you can find that is realistic and true. For example:

> *"Your dog will come home from the vet on Thursday."*
>
> *"Your dad will want to visit with you this weekend."*
>
> *"We have an appointment next Wednesday."*
>
> *"Your sister's birthday party is next month."*

F Get the FAMILY involved

Alert the parents of the seriousness of this occurrence and of your concerns. There are few more important reasons for a family to rally around one of its members than the prospect of an imminent death.

A Establish an APPOINTMENT

The student should not leave your presence without a slip of paper giving the date, time, and location of an appointment with a skilled mental health professional, appropriate social agency, or crisis service. Don't tell the student to make an appointment for help. Make the appointment while the student is still in your presence.

C Secure a CONTRACT

Obtain a *no suicide* contract, pact, or written agreement in which the student promises to postpone the suicide decision until some time in the future. Encourage a delay that would allow opportunities for the student to meet with a social agency or mental health professional.

T Arrange 24-hour support

Provide the student with the phone number of a crisis service or individual who agrees to be personally available (not just an answering machine) to talk with the student on an emergency basis at any time during the immediate future.

Address Self-Esteem

Positive self-esteem is of paramount importance for personal change. The student must conclude that he/she deserves the improvements your counseling efforts are designed to help bring about. Help the avoidant student become aware of his/her underlying beliefs about his/her level of personal incompetence. Then provide the student with means to move those beliefs in a positive direction.

A journal will help. Any student can keep a journal. A diary is totally private; a journal—which is shared with the counselor—is much more useful. Simply tell the student to include three types of entries:

What I did: The student records planned and unplanned experiences and the activities in which he/she participated.

How I felt: The student records the feelings he/she had immediately before, during, and after each event in the journal.

What I learned: The student includes how he/she processed each experience. He/she doesn't have to claim that every experience teaches him/her new things. He/she may indicate things he/she remembered by virtue of having an experience.

Ask the student to keep a journal of experiences during which any discouraging thoughts entered his/her mind. Twice each week for several weeks, discuss with the student what appears in the journal. Focus on how to turn mistakes and negative thoughts into positives and growth experiences. Discuss how the student could improve his/her response or interpretation if each event were to recur. Focus on what he/she could say or do differently. Remember that talking about the future is always safe and effective. It is the only time in which the student can make an improvement.

Surround With Encouragement

The student who is pursuing this goal of misbehavior is generally the most discouraged about him/herself and about life. Arrange to have uplifting and affirming posters hung on the wall of the student's room and beside his/her mirror. Consider some sort of daily affirmation or uplifting message, perhaps in a small bedside book or on a calendar. Make a standing appointment to talk briefly with the student every day about how things are going, even if it seems to be little more than exchanging greetings.

Refute Perfectionism

This student is intimidated by the prospect of making a mistake. Being terrified of not looking graceful, he/she is easily embarrassed about what might appear to be unsuccessful efforts at just about anything. The net result is an *If I can't do it perfectly, I won't even try* defeatist attitude. The best way to attack this perfectionism is to demote mistakes from the high status the student gives them to a more mundane, commonplace level. The basic goal is to convince the student that everyone makes mistakes and that there is no need to go to extraordinary lengths to avoid the risk of making one. Instruct the student in the eight healthy mistake-processing strategies summarized by the acronym *DELICATE* (see page 91).

Mistakes Are...

By John F. Taylor, Ph.D.

D **Decreasing**

"Look how far you've come."
"Things will get easier as you continue to practice."

E **Expected**

"That's why pencils have erasers."
"Everybody makes mistakes."
"Nobody's perfect."

L **Learning Opportunities**

"Success means any forward progress."
"What can you learn from this experience?"
"The only difference between a stumbling block and a stepping stone is how you use it."

I **Incompletions**

"You didn't run out of talent, you just ran out of time."
"You're just not done with this yet."
"Let's work on this again later."

C **Caused**

"Let's see what's giving you the trouble here."
"Every mistake has a cause."

A **Accidental**

"You can't do a mistake on purpose."
"All mistakes are accidents."

T **Temporary**

"You're just not ready for this right now."
"Maybe you can do better later."

E **Effort Indications**

"Mistakes prove you're trying."
"Mistakes are benchmarks on the path of effort."

Organize For School Success

See that the student has an alarm clock, notebook, suitable place for study, calendar, small chalkboard or corkboard for keeping track of appointments, desk or drawer for important papers and writing supplies, and any other components he/she needs to attend school.

Choose *Caution* Over *Fear*

When a situation appears challenging, this student pursues the fear option. Explain the distinction between *caution* and *fear.* Make a copy of *Fear vs. Caution* (page 93) for the student. Challenge him/her to use this list as a guide and make a personal project out of selecting the *caution option* over the *fear option.* I suggest a counseling homework assignment to keep a journal with at least one entry per day in which the student describes a potentially challenging situation, indicates what a fear-based response would be, and indicates what a caution-based response would be. The student should also enter what action was actually taken.

Discourage Shallow Entertainments

Find ways to involve this student in creative, constructive ways to spend time. Perhaps you can enroll him/her in a class that expects he/she will invest extra time in doing something active and interesting. An example would be an extra-credit project in a class such as mechanics, woodworking, or art. Extracurricular clubs and groups are also, of course, a prime opportunity for this kind of enrichment and energy diversion. Sitting in front of mindless television evening after evening or spending hours with pointless computer entertainment does little good. Actually accomplishing something, as with arts and crafts while listening to an entertaining CD, would be a much better investment that would pay rich dividends in improved coping energy and heightened self-confidence.

Arrange An *Accomplishments Vase*

Most people list things to do, then cross them off as they are accomplished. Students pursuing the avoidance goal of misbehavior typically don't even get as far as making a list. The solution is to invite the student to use a different method of regaining a grip on accomplishing day-to-day tasks. There is no written list of things to do. Ask the student to obtain an attractive, transparent vase. Early each morning, before launching the day, the student writes on note cards all activities that he/she is to accomplish that day. At the end of the day, the student puts each card describing an accomplishment into the vase. Unaccomplished items are carried over into the next day's card pile. The student should include such mundane accomplishments as bathing, dressing, and eating meals.

What builds up in the transparent vase is undeniable evidence that shouts back to the student: "Look what you've accomplished!" Have the student bring the vase and its contents to you every so often. Invite him/her to describe each accomplishment to you, thereby allowing him/her to further own and claim it. Gradually, this powerful therapeutic process can have a profound, uplifting effect.

Children and Teens Turn Their Fear into Caution

FEAR

1. Stagnates, immobilizes, inhibits
2. Induces more danger and risk
3. Person becomes more discouraged
4. Magnifies suffering and worry
5. Person wishes to control others
6. Withdrawal from and avoidance of challenge
7. Based on and feeds on ignorance
8. Hypothetical "What if..."
9. Fosters pessimism
10. Person feels powerless

CAUTION

1. Stimulates action, energizes
2. Reduces danger and risk
3. Person becomes encouraged
4. Decreases suffering and worry
5. Person focuses on controlling self
6. Approach and confronting of challenge
7. Based on and feeds on knowledge
8. Realistic "What is..."
9. Fosters optimism
10. Person feels powerful

Teacher Interventions For The Avoidant Student

Because many indications of avoidant misbehavior often involve easily detected underproductivity at school, there is much a caring teacher can do to assist.

Maintain Courtesy

The teacher should focus on facilitating positive changes in the student. He/she should never apply a psychiatric label, no matter how accurate, to any student in the presence of other students. The teacher can earn the student's trust by honoring confidentiality and helping prevent embarrassment.

Arrange Signals

Helpful assertion for this type of student involves being able to inform the teacher whenever an assignment is too difficult. The student should be given clear opportunity to request extra time for completing an assignment or assigned a partner with whom to share the project. A simple method is the colored card, which the student can flash to the teacher as a signal that means "May I please confer with you after class about this assignment?" After class, the teacher can provide clarification, help the student learn how to do the assignment, or make some sort of necessary modification.

Encourage "Study Buddies"

Help the student find ways to make studying more palatable. Studying with a partner is often more enjoyable than studying alone. Partners can take turns reading their class notes to each other. A variation is for each to read aloud from the other's notes. The student can make a game of studying with one or more friends. How about composing a mock quiz show on the spur of the moment, formulating the questions from class lecture notes? Classmates who answer and compose questions will benefit from the shared knowledge and are likely to perform well on any test covering that material.

Find Meaning In Assignments

Work to make assignments more relevant and interesting. Introduce the notion that the student has the ultimate responsibility for finding the material's relevance. In other words, it is not the teacher's responsibility to make every lesson exhilarating and fun. Life includes many boring moments and arduous times. Having introduced this first step, it is easy to proceed to the next step: challenging the student to generate meaning and relevance. Perhaps you can challenge the student to explain how a given assignment can be helpful or, conversely, how ignorance of the material in that assignment might result in negative experiences in the future.

Find Interest Areas

The teacher might be able to invite the avoidant student to bring to school products that were generated, constructed, or purchased as part of his/her hobby. Perhaps the student can give a brief report or speech about some aspect of the hobby. In this way, the teacher can become familiar with these areas of special opportunity for bolstering feelings of success.

Use Care In Grading

Grading of schoolwork represents a significant threat to any student with fragile self-esteem. There is a certain blow to self-confidence associated with receiving a grade that indicates fair to poor value. A student who routinely produces mediocre work is neither particularly enlightened nor uplifted by yet another *C* or *D*. Try to cushion this type of stress. Giving low grades simply pours salt on the avoidant student's emotional wounds. Research validates the common sense that a teacher's encouraging remarks, written as an accompaniment to the grade, are effective in bolstering a discouraged student. The statements should express faith in the student's ability, acknowledge effort shown, and draw attention to the strengths and correct aspects of the schoolwork the student has turned in. They must be real and credible, of course, and reserved for performances in which the student would not dismiss them as lies.

Address Areas Of Academic Stress

Use the *Taylor Academic Problem Identification Checklist* (page 96) to focus on the most crucial areas of academic difficulty for the student. Then arrange appropriate structuring, assistance, and remediation to bolster those areas.

The teacher's review of basic study skills, guided in part by the results of *The Taylor Academic Problem Identification Checklist* survey form, is always helpful.

The teacher can take a few moments to discuss specific helps for whatever aspects of classroom performance seem to be lagging. Perhaps the avoidant student doesn't know how to take good notes or how to study effectively for tests. A friendly conversation providing a few suggestions along these lines can go a long way toward rekindling academic interest.

THE TAYLOR ACADEMIC PROBLEM IDENTIFICATION CHECKLIST

Name of Student ______________________________

Name of Person Completing Form ______________________________

(CAREFULLY READ EACH ITEM BELOW AND CHECK ANY SUSPECTED PROBLEM AREAS.)

ATTENDANCE

- ☐ Attends scheduled classes
- ☐ Arrives at school on time
- ☐ Arrives at classes on time
- ☐ Sits in proper location when classes begin
- ☐ Remains alert, not sleepy

COMPREHENSION

- ☐ Understands a simple request the teacher is making
- ☐ Remembers what is heard
- ☐ Remembers what is read
- ☐ Remembers what is seen
- ☐ Reads, understands, and follows simple written instructions
- ☐ Understands and follows simple spoken instructions
- ☐ Understands and follows two-or three-step spoken instructions

ATTENTION CONTROL

- ☐ Remains on-task long enough to complete the task
- ☐ Works on seatwork, without assistance, for an acceptable length of time

ACADEMIC SKILLS

- ☐ Reads aloud with acceptable accuracy and speed
- ☐ Reads silently with acceptable understanding and speed
- ☐ Remembers the content of passages read silently
- ☐ Tells time on a non-digital timepiece
- ☐ Remembers the content of passages read aloud
- ☐ Has an acceptable speaking vocabulary
- ☐ Has an acceptable reading vocabulary
- ☐ Uses correct spelling of words
- ☐ Has an acceptable comprehension vocabulary
- ☐ Shows correct use of language

EMOTIONAL CONTROL

- ☐ Cooperatively handles transitions between different activities
- ☐ Accepts disciplinary consequences of negative behavior
- ☐ Responds appropriately to teacher reminders/ warnings
- ☐ Doesn't argue about and challenge rules
- ☐ Displays self-confidence
- ☐ Isn't easily discouraged

COURTESY

- ☐ Obtains the teacher's help by correct means
- ☐ Obtains the teacher's help at correct times
- ☐ Is courteous and friendly toward the teacher
- ☐ Doesn't talk back to the teacher

PRODUCTIVITY

- ☐ Meets due dates for daily assignments
- ☐ Meets due dates for short-term (less than one week) assignments
- ☐ Meets due dates for long-term assignments
- ☐ Uses good study habits
- ☐ Shows interest in academic work
- ☐ Shows interest in grades
- ☐ Brings needed materials to classes
- ☐ Participates in class discussions
- ☐ Becomes absorbed and interested in learning
- ☐ Tries hard on assigned seatwork
- ☐ Completes assignments
- ☐ Turns in neat, orderly, legible assignments
- ☐ Perseveres and doesn't give up on work
- ☐ Takes pride in work done
- ☐ Accepts challenges and follows through on hard assignments

PROBLEM-SOLVING

- ☐ Organizes and approaches tasks efficiently
- ☐ Uses good problem-solving and decision-making skills
- ☐ Asks for help when encountering problems
- ☐ Plans steps to reach academic goals

Teach Task-Approach Skills

Task-approach training is also helpful. Perhaps the teacher can help the student learn about managing time and pacing energy to accomplish challenging tasks. Most avoidant students do better if they work for brief periods—20–30 minutes, for example—then take a short break.

The *three strikes plan* is a helpful arrangement, especially for students who are quick to give up when coming upon a difficult problem. The student makes two attempts with a time limit, such as 60 or 90 seconds, for each attempt. After these two attempts, the student doesn't strike out by trying a third time. A study buddy, a family member, or the teacher helps him/her solve that problem.

Any student's ability to stay organized starts with his/her notebook.

Arrange An Organized Notebook

Helping the student prepare an organized notebook that facilitates study and learning is another service the teacher might perform. Any student's ability to stay organized starts with his/her notebook. Avoid a collection of portfolios. All of those pockets become hiding places for lost assignments.

The standard three-ring notebook serves well. Limit the available space for holding loose papers to an envelope taped to the inside of the back cover. For the most part, this envelope should hold completed homework that hasn't yet been turned in. Include a homework assignment sheet inside the front cover or a commercially available homework-organizing mini-notebook that fits into a three-ring notebook. A zipper pouch is useful for holding pencils, pens, erasers, sharpeners, ruler, tissues, lunch tickets, and other necessities. A portable three-hole paper punch that fits into a standard three-ring notebook can help prevent the student from losing important papers distributed to the class by the teacher. The student punches three holes in everything the teacher distributes and immediately puts the material into the notebook.

Teach Simplified Note Taking

Efficient note taking is essential if the student is to survive academically. For the avoidant student, I suggest a note-taking method that involves writing a minimum number of words and phrases, convenient use of symbols and abbreviations, minimal need for accuracies of grammar or punctuation, and a high percentage of future test questions. It is best if the student sits near the teacher rather than far back into the classroom.

Have the student take notes on 4" x 6" cards held together with small metal or plastic rings obtained at any office supply store. Tell the student to write one concept or idea on each card. Most tests will include something from one of five categories in the teacher's lectures. These categories are easy to remember because they spell the acronym *BROIL*. The student should write on a card anything the teacher:

- **B** writes on the **BOARD**
- **R** **REPEATS** during the lecture
- **O** says will be **ON** the test
- **I** indicates is **IMPORTANT**
- **L** presents as a **LIST** of two or more items

In addition to lectures, the student should focus on likely test questions in such assigned reading material as the textbook, a reading assignment, or information distributed to the class by the teacher. Four tip-offs indicate something the teacher will put on the next test. The student should copy anything that qualifies under these four categories on his/her study cards. The categories are easy to remember because they spell the acronym LOTS:

- **L** **LISTS** of any kind; two or more of anything
- **O** **ONE** test item hiding in each paragraph
- **T** **TEACHER** specifies it will be on the test
- **S** **SPECIAL** print, such as *bold-face* or *italic*

In this streamlined method, studying for tests becomes a matter of memorizing information on the cards. Reciting the information out loud is more effective than reading it silently. Several short review periods are better than one long review period prior to the test. The student can study with friends, reading aloud and quizzing each other until they have memorized the information on all the cards.

The cards can be removed from their rings and put into two piles: *I have learned this* and *Do again.* The student keeps self-quizzing until all the cards are in the *I have learned this* pile.

Getting a good night's sleep and arising early for last-minute review is better than staying up late the night before a test and trying to take the test on inadequate sleep.

Address Seatwork And Homework

Use the *Taylor Classroom Daily Report Form* (page 99) to maintain close communication between teacher and parent about the student's daily level of academic performance. If the student is especially disorganized about coming to class prepared and turning homework in on time, consider using this form. The teacher signs it and sends, faxes, or e-mails it to the parent each day. The parent may sign the form and return it to the teacher by the same means.

THE TAYLOR CLASSROOM DAILY REPORT FORM

Student ______________________________ Date __________

	YES	NO	COMMENTS
BEHAVIOR			
Did my child:			
arrive on time?	☐	☐	____________
bring needed materials?	☐	☐	____________
remain on task?	☐	☐	____________
participate appropriately?	☐	☐	____________
behave correctly?	☐	☐	____________
SCHOOLWORK			
Did my child:			
complete seatwork today?	☐	☐	____________
get a homework assignment?	☐	☐	____________
Did my child turn in:			
homework on time?	☐	☐	____________
homework that was neat?	☐	☐	____________
homework that was complete?	☐	☐	____________
homework that was properly headed?	☐	☐	____________
homework done according to directions?	☐	☐	____________

Overdue or incomplete work still out: ______________________________

____

Homework given today: ______________________________

____

Additional comments: ______________________________

____

____

My initials here ________ **indicate a request for contacting me by:**

- ☐ **e-mail** ______________________________
- ☐ **texting** (__________) ______________________
- ☐ **phone** (__________) ______________________

Please call me on______________ between the hours of ________ and ________.

Teacher's signature ______________________________

Parent/Guardian's signature ______________________________

Assist With Homework

Seatwork at school is much easier to monitor than homework. Helping an avoidant student with homework usually involves coordinating with a parent. Sometimes, however, working directly with the student may suffice. Start by inventorying the breakdown points between the teacher announcing a homework assignment and the student turning in the completed work.

Find ways to streamline the process and repair any glitches in these steps:

At school, the student:

- realizes an assignment is being given
- writes down the assignment correctly
- understands what the assignment is
- understands how to do the assignment correctly
- leaves school with needed texts and materials
- arrives home with the same materials

At home, the student:

- begins the homework session
- works on the homework until it is finished
- checks the homework for completeness, neatness, and accuracy
- puts the checked homework into the homework pocket
- leaves home with the notebook (and homework pocket)

Back at school, the student:

- arrives at school with the notebook
- keeps track of the homework until the correct class
- turns homework in on time

Whether or not a parent is also involved, the student should have a quiet, protected place devoted exclusively to study. His/her chair should be straight-backed with just a little padding, and he/she should sit upright while doing homework. All study supplies should be conveniently available near the study desk. The desk should be uncluttered. Background music is acceptable.

Breaking long or complicated assignments into smaller units and allowing more time for their completion are simple steps any teacher can take. These maneuvers can provide that extra boost to a discouraged, avoidant student having trouble turning in homework in a timely manner. Asking the student to work 15 minutes per night on lengthy assignments allows good pacing of effort without overwhelming the student.

Completed homework should always be placed in the homework pocket inside the notebook's back cover. The notebook should be placed near the door so the student won't forget to take it to school.

How To Counsel The Stimulation-Seeking Student

Stimulation-seeking misbehavior indicates a certain emptiness and aimlessness. The best therapeutic approach is to provide meaning, fulfillment, and truly exciting activities that quench the thirst for excitement.

Give The Lose–Lose Insight

Discuss with the student the various disruptive antics he/she is using to try to relieve boredom. Show the student how his/her disruptive misbehavior eventually gets him/her into trouble and makes it even more difficult for him/her to attend school and function in the school environment. Classmates will eventually tire of the student's disruptions, and teachers will become alienated from and disgusted with him/her. The student is literally creating the kind of classroom environment that is impossible to enjoy.

Suggest Win–Win Options

Here are some general forms of intervention for redirecting the extra energy the stimulation-seeking student seems to not know how to channel.

A Busy Schedule

Work with the student's parents and teachers to keep the student scheduled, busy, and actively engaged. Increase involvement with structured groups, music or dance lessons, programs, athletics, hobbies, Scouts, or similar preoccupations.

Practical Athletics

These activities, which don't require structured practices, are available at a moment's notice. Examples include swimming, skating, skateboarding, bicycling, weight lifting, jogging, gymnastics, tennis, basketball, and similar activities that don't require much athletic skill or advance preparation.

A Fun Idea List

Work with parents to develop a list of fun activities the student can enjoy whenever boredom starts to set in. The list should be displayed prominently in the student's home, and the student can consult it for ideas about what to do at any time. You can download from http://www.ADD-Plus.com a free master list from which any family can customize a fun idea list.

Arts And Crafts

Few enterprises are as rewarding or as time-effective for an easily bored and stimulation-seeking child as arts and crafts. With literally hundreds of forms, materials, projects, and aspects available to choose from, these activities provide a kaleidoscope of wholesome, entertaining, and fulfilling ways to help the student feel excited and gain a sense of accomplishment.

Regular Exercise

Burning off extra energy while getting stronger and improving overall health and coordination is an attractive set of outcomes for any student. Regular exercise can't help but decrease tendencies to misbehave for excitement's sake. Organized programs such as weight-loss exercise groups, martial arts training, and dance lessons are fine to consider.

Weekly Captivating Activity

In addition to practical athletics and regular exercise, find an exciting activity that involves rapid movement, adventure, exploration, and exhilaration for the student. The activity must be legal and something to which the student looks forward with great anticipation each week. Consider rock climbing, canoeing, rafting, surfing, water sports, boating, horseback riding, bungee jumping, sky diving, motocross, mountain biking, long-distance hiking, paintball, go-carts, snow boarding, or similar activities.

Social Skills

The reason the stimulation-seeking student feels so empty inside usually has to do with lack of fulfilling interpersonal relationships and lack of a sense of social enmeshment with peers. All the recommendations for working with the interaction-seeking misbehaving student may be helpful.

Teacher Interventions For The Stimulation-Seeking Student

The approaches the teacher might use for this type of student are the same as those for the interaction-seeking student. Help find ways to involve the student more directly in class activities and in contact with other students.

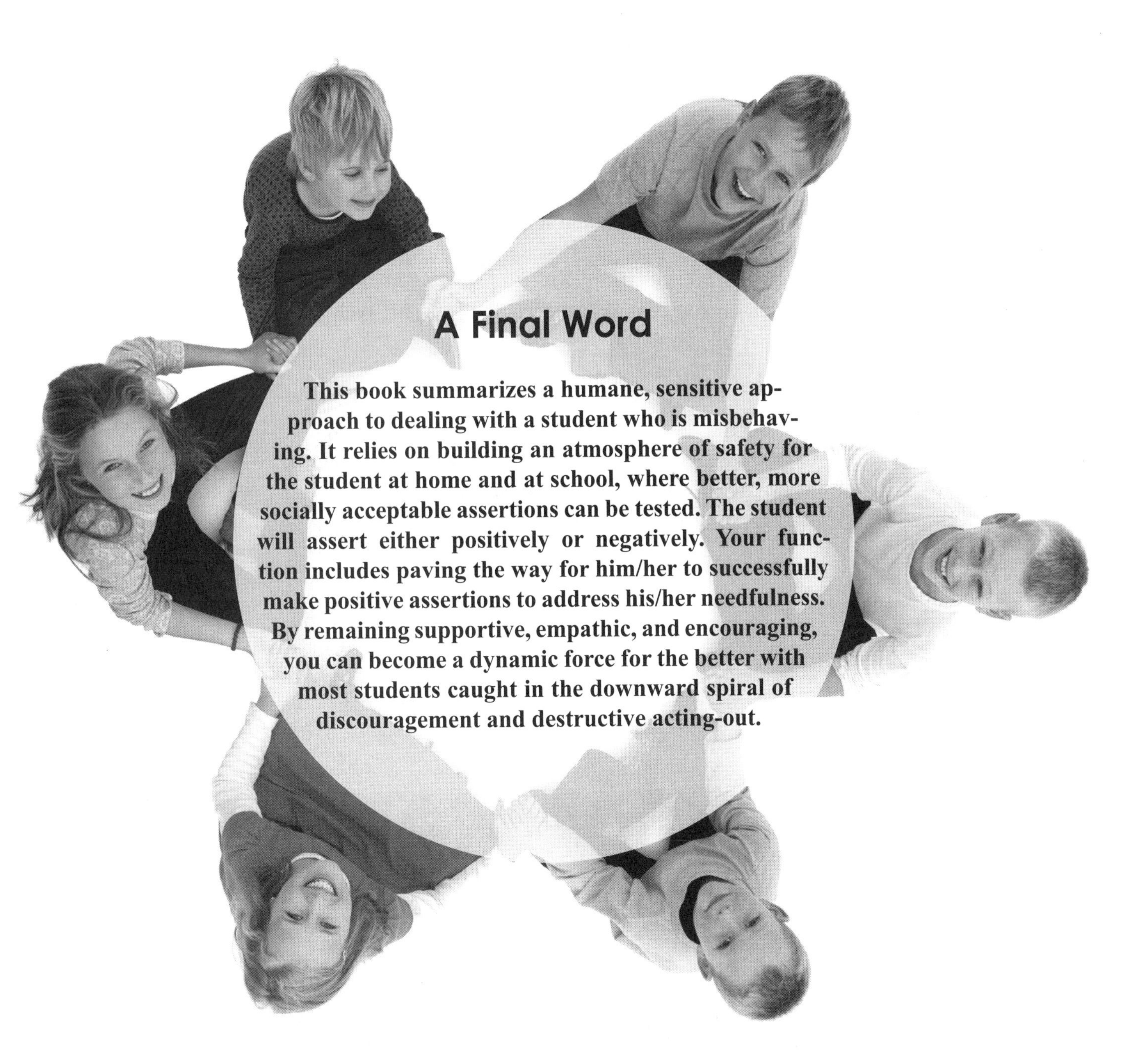

A Final Word

This book summarizes a humane, sensitive approach to dealing with a student who is misbehaving. It relies on building an atmosphere of safety for the student at home and at school, where better, more socially acceptable assertions can be tested. The student will assert either positively or negatively. Your function includes paving the way for him/her to successfully make positive assertions to address his/her needfulness. By remaining supportive, empathic, and encouraging, you can become a dynamic force for the better with most students caught in the downward spiral of discouragement and destructive acting-out.

John F. Taylor

John F. Taylor, Ph.D. is a family psychologist and Gestalt psychotherapist. He has produced many well-respected works, including *Helping Your ADD Child, The Survival Guide for Kids with ADD or ADHD, The School Success Tool Kit, From Defiance to Cooperation,* and numerous other books, booklets, videos, and CDs.

Dr. Taylor's resources may be accessed from his Web site:

http://www.ADD-Plus.com